MA

WOR

CW00739957

Mike Heath

Pumpkins, silly boy, pumpkins!

A Lifelong Fan's Appreciation of THE ROLLING STONES

© 2022 **Europe Books**| London
www.europebooks.co.uk | info@europebooks.co.uk

ISBN 979-12-201-2943-5
First edition: September 2022

Pumpkins, silly boy, pumpkins!

Preface

I started to write this book about The Rolling Stones seriously during their "50 & Counting Tour" in late 2013 though, in reality, I had commenced this labour, in my head, almost as soon as I had become smitten with the group right from the very start in the early 1960s. The reason that it has taken much longer than I thought is chiefly because I had not been subject to the strict rules that professional writers work to themselves. I had lots of other things to do like being a full-time teacher for thirty seven years and it was usually in stolen moments that I devoted time to the words that I wanted to write. When we moved to Greece in January 2007 to our newly built house with its two thousand square metre plot, it took up much of our time getting the garden and the olive trees sorted to our satisfaction. It felt guilty to be spending time on this when I could be weeding or planting or picking the array of citrus fruit from our trees or our olives. Any way it is now finished for your perusal.

This introduction has replaced the original one several times over. I am not deeply obsessive about the group but would describe myself as a strongly avid fan. What do you mean there is no difference? I do get daily updates via Google Alert for The Rolling Stones which help to keep me in touch with what is happening particularly when there is a tour or even a record or DVD due.

I have always felt that despite their highly global success that they are still not as revered as they ought to be especially in their native UK. Many people obsess about The Beatles and fail to appreciate the complexities of *my* favourite group. I have always tried to spread the gospel according to Jagger and Richards and this book will hopefully show just how much their music and their lives have impinged on my life and how much they mean to me and hopefully in other peoples' eyes.

I have always chosen or favoured strong and/or controversial larger than life types, to use the old cliché, as heroes. I hesitate to say role models because I have never really aspired to be anyone other than me. The Rolling Stones have always been my heroes.

I find the current preoccupation with celebrity laughable or should I say those who believe that they are celebrities; the sort of people who become famous (usually albeit fleetingly) solely because they have acquired some sort of fame. I am referring to the ones who appear on reality TV shows like "Celebrity Big Brother" or "I'm A Celebrity, Get Me Out Of Here", usually to revive a flagging career.

The Rolling Stones have endured for six decades and show few signs of stopping. Even the serious health problems suffered by Ronnie Wood and Mick Jagger and the occasional mishaps for Keith Richards haven't dented their progress. The very sad demise of Charlie Watts, their gentleman drummer, seems to have reinvigorated the group as their No Filter USA tour of 2021 has shown.

They have adapted their music over time to keep at least a modicum of whatever the contemporary scene was. They are deeply ingrained in the music world but to me are much bigger than that. Wherever you go in the world there will be somebody, who, has not only heard of them, but, is a fan. Since the demise of The Beatles, at the very end of the sixties, I feel that The Stones have been taken for granted by too many people – almost to the point of being dismissed. They were the first true influencers of rock culture. The Beatles were purveyors of pop music beautifully shaped by George Martin. The Rolling Stones became 'the greatest rock band in the world'. At the forefront of the renegade generation, they influenced those that followed through their fashion, lyrics and raw showmanship. This book is all about why they mean so much to me and why they deserve an even greater recognition than they already have.

A friend who read through a rough draft of this book said that she thought that it was aimed primarily at white men of a similar age to me (old) and did not give enough detail about some things that nonfans would not know The Redlands raid is an example. There was an element of truth to this which I then set about rectifying. It is true that I am writing for existing fans and those who know of the exploits of the group but I would say that, while I did not intentionally set out to write the story of The Rolling Stones, (there are many books that do that already), I was hoping that as I explained why I liked the band and its achievements, it might gain new fans along the way – especially younger ones. While the hits of the mid 60s had secured their stardom, it was the time during the late '60s and early '70s that would secure the crown for the Stones as creative legends. It is this that I celebrate. Those who were surprised to learn things that they did not know, can now appreciate what I liked and, therefore, share in the resultant enjoyment. I said at the beginning that I used to be a teacher. Consider this, also then, as a teaching aid for the uninitiated.

Introduction

The Stones have been a part of my life for almost sixty years. I tend to see things in clear black and white and rarely in grey. The Stones have been larger than life almost from the start, thanks, in no small part, to their first manager Andrew Loog Oldham. He produced an image of the group that had a certain resonance with a fifteen year old boy who was well and truly into music in what was to become a most vibrant decade – The Sixties. Living in Peterborough, as a grammar school student at an all-boys school, I rarely got to glimpse the Swinging Sixties (well, never really!) as they became known - apart from on TV.

The stories that emanated from the press in those early days, and in the music papers like *NME* and *Melody Maker* and, later, *Sounds*, served to conjure up a world that I wanted to know more about. The Stones, in a small way, were my proxies in all of this. Though I have never even had a cigarette or indulged in many of the excesses that they were reported to have experienced, nor had any real desire to do so either, it was still a world that I found fascinating. Sex, drugs and Rock 'n' Roll by proxy. It was always destined to be so. Sad but true. Well, actually - just true.

Coming from an era where adherence to rules was expected and quite strictly enforced, the stance adopted by The Rolling Stones was a breath of fresh air to a young teenage boy like me. At Deacon's School in Peterborough, you would be prevented, by the ever-officious prefects, from entering the school hall for morning assembly if your tie was incorrectly knotted. The prefects would also watch for those who, on their way to school, were not wearing their school cap properly or, sin itself, not even sporting it at all. I recall being admonished by a teacher because my sideboards were approaching the level below the bottom of my ears. I was told that it was a Teddy Boy trait and that they had to be shortened forthwith. I had started shaving just before my fifteenth birthday and, in this newly grown-up activity, I used to leave a miniscule extra tenth of an inch of sideboard each time I shaved. I had hoped that it would be noticed by my peers but not by the teachers, most of whom sported the traditional short back and side's haircut or were balding. All of the staff were male. The only females in the school were the Head Master's secretary and the caretaker's wife who lived on site.

When I retired from teaching a few years ago, the sixth formers could, and often did, wear moustaches and beards as well as a myriad of hairstyles long and short. One of our Sixth Formers chose a reverse way to demonstrate his feelings. He wore a school blazer and certainly stood out amongst the mufti of all the others. In my day very few dreamed of making any comment. Times have certainly changed. The petty restrictions of yesteryear have all but been swept away. My world in 1962/63 was certainly different and any chance to mount a challenge to authority was gladly seized upon. The Stones anti-establishment stance was a resonant tonic. Rebellion in my school was hardly of the proportions of the Lindsay Anderson film "If" but if any opportunity arose then it would be willingly embraced.

I remember that we all had to wear short trousers in the first year at age eleven. Long trousers were the prerogative of second years and above. The wearing of school caps was relaxed after leaving the fifth year. It was always greeted, on the last day of term at the end of that year, with a ceremonial bonfire in the playground of the cursed headwear.

This must sound very trivial but at the time it was an important issue to us all. Oddly enough I could always imagine Brian Jones in his school uniform, striped blazer and cap. He had that aura of posh boy even though his lifestyle legislated against that.

One thing that I, and certainly others, enjoyed and even revelled in, was the notoriety that was associated with The Stones. Mojo magazine has a feature each month where three music celebrities go "All Back To My Place" and answer a regular set of questions. One, which I always look at is "What was the first record you bought? And where did you buy it?" I check to see how many choose Rolling Stones records. In the April 2018 issue Al Jourgensen from the group Ministry answers thus: *December's Children* by The Rolling Stones. But I didn't buy it, I stole it from a Sears in Arlington Heights, Chicago. I was seven or eight, and I managed to slip it under my jacket. Why the Stones? They were on the radio in the car ride over and my parents said, "This stuff sucks, they're ruining our society."

This makes sense to me. It was a way to get back at the older generation who just did not get it. My parents, especially my mother, most certainly did not.

Thinking back to my own school days, I had an early Rolling Stones link even that I did not know at the time. I used to sit next to a boy called Paul Jeffreys in most lessons, as we were sat alphabetically. He spent most of every lesson drawing guitars in biro at the back and on the covers of his exercise books. Despite frequent teacher tellings-off, he continued with this. He was really into music and, not unexpectedly, guitar playing. I often wonder what happened to him as he did not stay on into the sixth form and the last I heard of him was that he was playing bass guitar in a night club in Rome.

The reason I remember him well is two-fold. In his front garden he once made a firework by putting explosives into a metal pipe, and, after igniting the fuse, he dropped it into a dustbin. They were always made of metal in those pre-wheelie bin days. I managed to run for cover, but he was much closer having lit the fuse. The explosion not only sounded magnificent but also shattered the metal bin. I had never heard the word lacerated before that time but soon became familiar with it as poor old Paul was off school for some time with lacerated buttocks. When he did return, he could only stand up in lessons for the first week or so. No one ever described the firework as a bomb but undeniably it was a form of pipe bomb even if, only part of, a schoolboy prank.

The main reason I remember Paul is that, in his guitar days, he was playing somewhere in the London area where the embryonic Rolling Stones were playing too. Not that we knew who they were then. He came back to school on the Monday morning with a black eye and a tale that he had had a fight over a girl with someone, who could only have been Brian Jones, which he claimed to have won. We were all very impressed and though we had no corroborative evidence it seemed more than likely from what we knew of both Paul and what he had heard about Brian. It was only later, after reading about The Rolling Stones, in their very early days, and Brian in particular, that we realised that his story was probably true.

The Rolling Stones were pilloried in the press as the personification of sexual freedom. They became heroes of their generation with their risqué lyrics and their plain old 'attitude'. Parents hated them. Grandparents, too – my grandmother, I recall, was very scathing in her verdict about this sort of music and their morals. They became the emblem of everything the establishment hated and feared. They were widely adored by the young at least those of my acquaintance. They were role models for a generation – for a counterculture. I remember Bill Wyman speaking on breakfast TV a few years ago claiming that their critics never talked about their music. They complained about their hair, their uncleanliness, their clothes, their looks. I never believed that. I liked them for their music and their attitude. In an increasingly affluent world that had shaken off the austerity of the 1950s, the young were gaining more independence and demanding a bigger say in everything. The Rolling Stones were at the forefront of this new attitude.

My early tastes in Music: I got into Jazz via the radio from AFN (American Forces Network) and from there, the short distance, into the blues at the age of fourteen. The Stones easily fitted into my musical psyche. I was never a big fan of a lot of the pop music at that time (moon and Junes), preferring instrumentals and especially guitar led music.

The Shadows, The Ventures, The Spotniks and The Tornadoes along with Duane Eddy were my scene. I was, however, a big fan of Del Shannon, partly because of the high-pitched organ instrumental breaks, and went with my schoolmate, Derek Wallace, to Leicester (The De Montfort Hall) by train at the age of fourteen, and again at fifteen, to see the *Runaway* star. There was not a parent in sight. How times have changed.

The first record I ever bought was *Dream Lover* by Bobby Darin. I bought it second hand, in 1959, from a school mate, Bob Taylor. It was his sister's record and I wondered if she knew. Her name E.Taylor was inscribed on the record and I did think of Elizabeth Taylor, who was a very leading celebrity at that time. I bought it because the flip side was a real rock n roll belter: *Bullmoose* - It heavily featured piano and saxophone. I also bought from him, a copy of Duane Eddy's *Peter Gunn*. Eddy was one of my very early heroes, too; so much so, that I had the words "till moons shall wax and wane no more" (from "Jesus Shall Reign") underlined in my school hymn book that was kept in the top pocket of my school blazer. It was this strong guitar music that I really liked. "The twang was the thang" as he put it.

I bought all of the Shadows singles as they were released. It was not a huge leap to the guitar-oriented music coming from The Rolling Stones. Hank Marvin was another guitar hero. Certainly, the earliest Stones records did not have the gravitas of their later music but I was hooked by their energy – their raw power. I bought *Come On*, a Chuck Berry cover, which became their first hit (June 1963), albeit only medium sized. I seem to remember that it entered the charts at number 23, and, despite being in the charts for about three months, only rose to number 20. But after this they never really looked back.

The slightly odd thing, to an outsider, about my very first purchases, is that we did not have a gramophone for another two years at home but I didn't want any of the music I had started to enjoy to pass me by. So I started collecting early. When we did get a gramophone I had quite a few singles ready to play. I bought a second hand Dansette record player for my bed room (pictured below).

My Dansette record player

My mum always disliked the noise ("jungle music" she nastily called it). I recall the self-penned Rolling Stones hit single *The Last Time* (1965) with its strident, repeated, guitar riff, as it slowly faded out, being particularly annoying to her, especially when I used to leave the arm off my record player so that it would play over and over again. I don't think my mother ever became a Rolling Stones fan. She did like The Beatles, however, especially "that nice looking Paul McCartney".

I have always been a huge music fan and have been very keen on quizzes and general knowledge. I put this down to my parents and the help they gave as I was learning especially while I was at Junior School. I was an inveterate reader. (They wouldn't buy a TV until I had passed my 11+. In later years I realised that this had to have been a financial rather than an ethical reason) I duly passed the exam but when they then bought the television – a good old Ferguson - my two younger brothers and sister were allowed to watch even though they had not taken the exam yet. I was very interested in all sorts of things. It was once I discovered the power that music can have over you - not just the words but the emotive nature of a particular riff (you can see where I am going with this), I became immersed in music. My mother used to say to me during my GCE years "If only you would put as much effort into your school work as you do for your music..." Well, mother, I think that I did. The music helped me. I found I could revise much better with music whether from crackly old Radio Luxembourg or from an LP or two. I followed this same path while doing my teacher training and again when pursuing an Open University degree in the late 70s to the early 80s. In fact one of the assignments I was able to set for myself during one particular popular culture module was to compare a Rolling Stones album with one by the Sex Pistols. (See Appendix A page 183).

The First Stones' Record

I bought the first Rolling Stones LP when it was released in 1964 for thirty two shillings, I think - well, it was probably 31/11d (£1.60 in today's money). Of course I had to save up in order to pay for it Most of my friends only bought singles as LPs were quite expensive. Marble Arch did have budget and sampler albums for sale at

18

about fifteen bob. I was able to purchase the Stones LP because I had a Saturday job for a couple of years at Crooks, Gentlemen's Outfitters, which was situated on the corner of Lincoln Road and Westgate in Peterborough. This, and particularly the second LP, formed the soundtrack to parties in those days.

Having seen The Rolling Stones on *Ready, Steady, Go* (*The Weekend Starts here...*) on a Friday evening, only served to amplify their appeal. The show was raw. You could see the cameras as they weaved in and out of the dancing throngs of young people. It was anything but smooth and that was its appeal. It looked and sounded real. Dance moves could be seen – they even used to have someone demonstrating the latest dance from America. The Stones appeared regularly as guests which was great, too.

The parties that I used to go to almost always had Rolling Stones LPs as the main music source. They were just great to dance to. I always associate the track *Play With Fire* which was the flip side of *The Last Time* and later released on *Out Of Our Heads* – the next LP to be issued also during 1965 - with a particular party at The Vicarage in Park Crescent. Smooching with Sarah. No, not the title of a record, but the name of my first, serious, girlfriend. Our school had links with an all- girls school in Peterborough for plays, debates, a film club (which I co-ran) and we use to socialise with them too. In truth, that was the main reason. A number of friendships were formed. Mine lasted till I went off to college. Whenever I hear that song, it always takes me back to that party.

Dave Foxley's party. Sarah and me on the extreme right

These two first Rolling Stones' albums had set the seal for me. The first was released in April 1964 (just in time

for my birthday) and the second, imaginatively named Rolling Stones Number 2 album, came out the following January. Two great albums within nine months. Brilliant. You cannot countenance groups, and, almost certainly, The Stones, bringing out music that rapidly in today's world.

Their first EP was excellent too. My copy is pictured below. It came out before Decca had let them release an LP. It was a very raw production with Bill's bass guitar standing out and driving the music onwards. I liked the Arthur Alexander song *You Better Move On*, another American favourite that the band had been doing in concert. It showed a softer, more lyrical and soulful side to their music. The intensity, however, is still present as in the harder edged rawness of the other three tracks. Another one for smooching with Sarah!

St●nes Miscellany #1

EP Tracks: 1. Bye Bye Johnny; 2. Money; 3. You Better Move On; 4. Poison Ivy

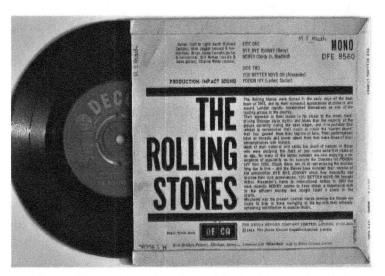

The Rolling Stones first LP sold 100,000 copies on its first day of release knocking The Beatles off the top of the charts. The front cover showed the five young men

looking very moody and surly. It did not have their name or the name of the record either. Only the Decca logo adorned the cover. This really helped to foster the kind of image that Andrew Loog Oldham was striving to project. In the comparisons with The Beatles, this was important. Legend has it that Lennon was probably more suited to the Oldham image in reality than any of the Stones, who many have remarked just how nice and refined they were after meeting them. Oldham, who was the instigator of the infamous press headline "Would you let your daughter go out with a Rolling Stone?" projected an arrogant, loutish, sexually marauding, anti-charismatic, working class persona for his protégés. This was very much in tune with the growing dissent within youth culture in society and was going to be played up to the full. The desexualised masculinity that was projected in the 1950's (Pat Boone, Paul Anka, Perry Como, Bobby Darin and Andy Williams et al) was the norm and was now being well and truly shattered.

The Pretty Things, The Animals and, to a lesser degree, Them, also followed the path that The Rolling Stones were stomping down. Not a surprise, then, that these happened to be my very favourite groups of the time. It was this rugged, almost ruthless, image that appealed to me. The fact that The Stones didn't wear a uniform but often turned up for gigs and didn't have to change from their ordinary clothes was a relief from the uniformity of most other groups at that time. Even at fifteen years of age, I could see through the conformity of neat suits. It was the music I wanted not fashion icons. The Stones, under Loog Oldham's influence, were breaking down the barriers. Anyone who knows me well, can verify that I have never harboured a yearning to be a fashionista. Fashion has occasionally caught up with me – never the other way round.

Controversy

One of the things that I like best about them is the controversy that has followed them for most of their lives. They appear to have always been "in it" for the music and prepared to stand up for themselves.

Controversy most of their lives - from peeing outside a petrol station and being fined, drug busts (genuine and not), album covers, lyrics and subject matter - politics, devil worship - real or imagined - figured heavily, too. I recall the press at the time claiming that the song *Midnight Rambler* had made a hero out of the Boston Strangler which resulted in not unsurprising complaints. I always looked out for their next "cocking a snoop" at the establishment. Videos that were rated 18 and lyrics that caused offence in an era well before the parental discretion sticker was introduced were welcomed by me. As one who, very largely, favours freedom of expression, and, by definition, therefore opposed to censorship, the Stones were blazing a trail for me and my fellow fans to follow. There is a line in *Jigsaw Blues* about being an outcast all of his life – for me, the Stones have deliberately set out to be outlaws and wallowed in it too.

As an example of the way that The Stones have sought to be deliberately provocative, you only need to look at the song entitled *Cocksucker Blues* (aka Schoolboy Blues). It was given, or rather thrust upon, London/Decca Records in 1970 by The Stones for their final single that they owed the label. Jagger penned the song deliberately to anger the executives at the record company. London/Decca unsurprisingly refused to release it. It was released in 1983 in West Germany on the album *The Rest of the Best* as a bonus single, but then dropped from the album after just four weeks. It features only Mick and Keith. There is, though, a bootleg of the song out there with the entire band playing on it, recorded sometime around the mid '70s.

The infamous, unreleased film documentary of the same name, chronicling The Rolling Stones' North American tour in 1972 in support of their album *Exile on Main St*, is probably even better known. Having obtained a bootleg copy you can see why it remains unreleased. There was much anticipation for the band's arrival in the United States, since they had not visited there since the 1969 disaster at the Altamont, in which a fan was stabbed and beaten to death by Hells Angels. Behind the scenes, the tour embodied debauchery, lewdness and hedonism. The film was shot in 'cinéma vérité' style, with several cameras available for anyone in the entourage to pick up and start shooting. The band, who had commissioned the film, decided that its content was embarrassing and potentially incriminating, and did not want it shown. The provocative title, nudity and drug use were enough to see that it was withdrawn much to the chagrin of Robert Frank, the director. The biter bit?

Lyrics to *Cocksucker Blues*:

> *Well, I'm a lonesome schoolboy*
> *And I just came into town*
> *Yeah, I'm a lonesome schoolboy*
> *And I just came into town*
> *Well, I heard so much about London*
> *I decided to check it out*

Well, I wait in Leicester Square
With a come-hither look in my eye
Yeah, I'm leaning on Nelsons Column
But all I do is talk to the lions
Oh where can I get my cock sucked?
Where can I get my ass fucked?
I may have no money,
But I know where to put it every time
Well, I asked a young policeman
If he'd only lock me up for the night
Well, I've had pigs in the farmyard,
Some of them, some of them, they're alright
Well, he fucked me with his truncheon
And his helmet was way too tight
Oh where can I get my cock sucked?
Where can I get my ass fucked?
I ain't got no money,
But I know where to put it every time
I'm a lonesome schoolboy in your town
I'm a lonesome schoolboy

A later controversy that still has a resonance today with the Me Too campaign came with the advertising for the *Black and Blue* album from 1976. The advertising for this record used model Anita Russell who proclaimed "I'm 'Black and Blue' from The Rolling Stones – and I love it." This billboard advert on Sunset Boulevard showed Russell as a bruised and bound woman sitting on the gatefold cover of the new album. Atlantic Records quickly pulled the advert but not before a number of very vocal women's groups complained in no uncertain terms. The WAVAW (Women Against Violence Against Women) actually used red paint to deface the billboard proclaiming, "This is a crime against women". While doing some research on another topic relating to censorship, I discovered this advert. I had to smile. This was well in keeping with the bad boy image. It is often said that there is no such thing as bad publicity and, even though this album is not as widely favoured as a number of others, this publicity, especially in the USA, cannot have harmed its fan base. Anita Russell, apparently, is quoted as saying that she didn't mind at all, and, in fact, was happy for the work... and for the money.

Black and Blue The Rolling Stones

Misogyny

Despite my overall admiration for Jagger, there is one area that now, well into the twenty first century, I do find difficult to fully support. Those critics, mainly female, point out the misogynistic and racial overtones of certain lyrics. Today (post the Weinstein scandal and the Me Too Movement) some of this will seem uncomfortable for many and, without taking sides, the excuse offered is that it was certainly of its time. What is now regarded as PC certainly was not at that time. The era of the swinging sixties and the seventies saw a breakthrough in sexual freedom in all areas of the arts. Film and music, in particular, saw the boundaries being pushed outwards. One example which would seem unthinkable today was the "work" of Cynthia Plaster Caster, who made plaster moulds of rock star's erect penises. Of course it was seen as bizarre by some but the whole world of the groupies was viewed as almost de rigueur.

There are a few Stones songs, that are still performed today, that have lyrics which cause outrage and offence to some women. *Brown Sugar*, a staple concert offering throughout their career, is a supreme case in point. It is the most popular song ever written about drugs, rape, cunnilingus and slavery:
"Gold Coast slave ship bound for cotton fields
Sold in the market down in New Orleans
Scarred old slaver knows he's doin' all right
Hear him whip the women just around midnight". These are the opening words to the song. There is some ambiguity in that one explanation is that brown sugar is actually heroin rather than black slave women. but that doesn't really wash. It's complicated. "God knows what I'm on about on that song," Jagger bluntly admitted in a 1995 talk with *Rolling Stone* magazine. "It's such a mishmash. All the nasty subjects in one go," he told *Rolling Stone* in 1995. "I would never write that song now." To their credit, the Stones have removed some of the more controversial lyrics from live performances, and they

replaced the "just like a Black girl should" line with the still not great "just like a young girl should" in subsequent recordings of the track. So, some editing has taken place over the years though this then gets into another potentially controversial area. He has also apologized when the subject comes up: "I didn't think about it at the time," Jagger told *Rolling Stone*. "I never would write that song now. I would probably censor myself. I'd think, 'Oh, God, I can't. I've got to stop.'"

Sometimes, though, words just mean what they mean, whether you want to admit it or not. It does what it says on the tin to use an old advertising mantra. There's a slave ship, a market, and a slaver, who's whipping the women and posing a question: "How come you taste so good?"

The words are problematic. Times have changed, without a doubt, but this song is far too ingrained within The Stones canon. You find yourself being swept so far away with the glorious music that you can excuse the words. This was always a record I would put on at parties in the 1970s to get people up and dancing. At a fellow teacher's party (Bob Davey), he came over to me and said "nobody is dancing". I took off his Carpenters LP and went straight for *Sticky Fingers* and Brown *Sugar*. Soon everyone was dancing. The power of the music took over and the lyrics were given a free pass. I am sure that this happened unconsciously as it continues to this day with many people liking the song without giving much real thought to the subject matter.

Keith Richards feels like critics of the song have missed the point. "You picked up on that, huh?" the guitarist told the *Los Angeles Times* about the set list omission on the 2021 No Filter tour. "I don't know. I'm trying to figure out with the sisters quite where the beef is. Didn't they understand this was a song about the horrors of slavery? But they're trying to bury it. At the moment I don't want to get into conflicts with all of this shit." Richards is still "hoping that we'll be able to resurrect the babe in her glory somewhere along the track."

Mick Jagger gave a more diplomatic explanation for excluding the song. "We've played 'Brown Sugar' every night since 1970, so sometimes you think, We'll take that one out for now and see how it goes," he said. "We might put it back in." Time will tell.

For the erstwhile so called 'bad boys of rock' to submit to self-censorship in light of the woke culture has been criticised by many commentators. Piers Morgan, whose views I often find myself opposed to, wrote a lengthy article for the MailOnline on 13 October 2021, calling it a cowardly climbdown especially as he took the view expressed by Keith Richards that it is an anti-slavery song.

Morgan takes the view that there ought to be campaigns about many of the rapper's songs and quotes a few: "Rappers also spew incredibly offensive lyrics about women. Snoop Dogg sang: 'B*itches ain't sh*t but hoes and tricks, lick on these nuts and suck the d*ck.' Kanye West sang: 'I know she like chocolate men, she got more n*ggas off than Cochran.' Eminem sang: 'Slut, you think I won't choke no whore, til the vocal cords don't work in her throat no more.'
And as for Pharrell Williams' Blurred Lines collaboration with Robin Thicke, he's since admitted the lyrics including 'I hate these blurred lines, I know you want it'

were 'rapey." There can be no doubt that many of these lyrics are seriously inflammatory and you could argue that just because this is clearly unpleasant that Jagger's lyrics are another matter altogether. Two wrongs do not make a right. On reflection I will say that the jury is still out on *Brown Sugar*. Part of me does wonder if this simply an exercise to keep the group in the news to boost ticket sales at what just might turn out to be the last USA tour.

It has to be noted that Rolling Stones fans were outraged at the decision to drop the song. Instagram was bombarded with fans who claimed that they did not understand the controversy as it is clearly an anti-slavery song and that artists should be free to express themselves without fearing 'cancel culture'.

There are, however, other songs in The Jagger/Richards repertoire that have caused consternation. One that women today object to is *Under My Thumb* from *Aftermath*. It is, without a doubt, The Stones' most sexist song. Again, the marimba and the fuzz bass guitar's insistent beat drive the song forward. It has always been another favourite with fans. The lyric is a sort of Taming Of the Shrew scenario with a pushy girl finally being controlled after dominating the male. She thought she was going to get the best of him, and now he's got her trained to the point of submission. It is unclear if this is sexual or just social submission. The language used compares the woman to a "pet", a "Siamese cat" and a "squirming dog" and this has provoked some negative reactions, especially amongst feminists, who objected to what they took as the suppressive sexual politics of the male. Like with *Some Girls* (see below), Jagger has insisted that *Under My Thumb"* is meant to be parody. "It's a bit of a jokey number, really," he told *Rolling Stone* in 1995. "It's not really an anti-feminist song any more than any of the others.Yes, it's a caricature, and it's in reply to a girl who was a very pushy woman." Still, he's tweaked it a bit since then, changing the references to the "girl" in its lyrics to "woman" in live performances. It is, undeniably, a very well-constructed song and, as I have commented, a fan favourite. I think many accept the tongue in cheek nature of the lyrics. Like *Brown Sugar* the song has been given a free pass. It was played ten times on the recent No Filter USA tour in 2019.

A third song written in the same year as *Under My Thumb* that also attracts the anti-misogynistic critics is *Stupid Girl*. At the time I regarded this as a tongue in cheek number. The list of faults the girl has are so numerous. I now believe that it is vindictive and probably written in retaliation to a failed relationship or even an anti-groupie diatribe,

"She's the worst thing in this world
Look at that stupid girl".

I don't believe that it is part of the repertoire anymore and regarded as yet another one deemed to be acceptable in those pre-PC days.

Also from this era the song *Stray Cat Blues* (1968) from *Beggars Banquet* features the lines:
"I can see that you're 15 years old
No, I don't want your I.D.,"

Jagger comments that this is neither a "hanging matter" nor a "Capital crime". He asks if she will bring her even wilder friend with her who can "join in, too" upstairs. On the highly successful live album *Get Yer Ya*

Yas Out Jagger changes her age to 13. Deliberately provocative or not?

The final song I have to mention is *Some Girls* (1978) from the eponymously titled album. It contains a catalogue of different racial types of girls with their particular idiosyncrasies. The infamous lines that always stand out to me are:

"Black girls just wanna get fucked all night
I just don't have that much jam"

I could hardly believe what I had heard, with its deliberate sense of mischievousness, let alone the obvious racial and misogynistic overtones. The ensuing media controversy was inevitable. Here we are back to the "no such thing as bad publicity" idea. Jagger is reported to have said that the song was basically a joke and black girl friends of his "just laughed". His lyrics make reference to French, Italian, American and English girls with their respective foibles. Finally Asian girls get a highly suggestive yet coded verse:

"Chinese girls are so gentle They're really such a tease You never know quite what they're cooking inside those silky sleeves"

I read a review once that called the song "...a sexist and racist horror..." and then, in vindication added "...it's also terrifically funny and strangely desperate in a manner that gets under your skin and makes you care". We are back to the acceptance theory here again.

In this age where celebrity rules the roost, any indiscretion becomes headline news. The Stones, almost from the start, revelled in scandal. Loog Oldham certainly ramped up the stories to help develop a certain dark image. Brian Jones fathered six children with various women which did not help his image much but played into the Loog Oldham overview.

Similarly, the then 47 year old Bill Wyman's liaison with a thirteen year old Mandy Smith, which led to an ill-fated marriage, later helped to reinforce the view that people had formed of The Rolling Stones. Do we turn a blind eye or do we turn against them? The screening in cinemas of Wyman's recent documentary *The Quiet One* (2019) was cancelled by some authorities as a result of his past Mandy episode. Claims of his past sexual predatory nature were given as the reason. I did meet and speak to Bill, who was with Mick Taylor, at a Rhythm Kings Concert outside the Cambridge Corn Exchange on the 29th November 2011.

This was the third time I had seen Bill Wyman's Rhythm Kings. They are a seasoned group of musicians who give the impression that they are really enjoying what they do. Bill was standing in the road outside the front of the Corn Exchange and there were four of us chatting to him. Mick Taylor, who was guesting with the group that evening, was also there but not pictured. He had a jacket with a long scarf wrapped around his neck. When we saw him on stage he had the same jacket and scarf on. I liked that. When The Stones first started they would turn up in the gear they were going to play in; a far cry from all the sharp suits that a lot of others wore on tour and on TV.

Bill confided to us that he was quitting smoking. He was known for wandering off stage from time to time during performances for a cigarette. I read in the national press later that week that he was indeed quitting smoking. We heard it first.

The performance of the group with people like Georgie Fame, Andy Fairweather Low, Albert Lee, Beverley Skeete and Frank Mead and Nick Payn (truly great horn players), Gary Brooker (ex Procol Harum), is always joyous. Among their wide repertoire of R 'n' B and Rockabilly there is always an occasional Rolling Stones song, too…and why not?

When The Stones started out were not that interested in convention nor fame. I heard a radio interview that Bill once gave where he said that the band often turned their backs to the audience and just played for themselves. This epitomises their profound love of the music right from the start and their outright cussedness which I found appealing.

Liaisons

Anita Pallenburg was one of Brian Jones's early partners but ended up with Keith. While a partner to Richards, during the making of the film *Performance*, it is rumoured that Jagger and Anita "spent the night together, as the song goes – at least according to Keith. With Mick Jagger, father of eight children, a major part of his reputation is as a ladies man. A modern-day lothario.

His time with Marianne Faithfull is well documented and he has had liaisons and dalliances with many women over the years. His first child Karis was with Marsha Hunt. He later married Bianca Pérez-Mora Macias and had a second child Jade. His long term "marriage" to Jerry Hall, whom he had 'taken' from Brian Ferry, produced four children Elizabeth, James, Georgia and finally Gabriel. One of the women with whom Jagger had an affair, while living with Hall, was Brazilian fashion model, Luciana Gimenez, who gave birth to the seventh son Lucas. L'Wren Scott a model and fashion designer met Jagger in Paris in 2001 and had a long standing relationship with him until she took her own life in 2014 following a period of depression.

In 2016, Jagger was already great-grandfather when his much younger ballerina girlfriend, Melanie Hamrick, produced his eighth child –a son Deveraux Octavian. Whatever verdict one comes up with about the modern day lothario that is Jagger, one can point to the fact that he is a dedicated and devoted father. A good family man. His love of his children certainly appears to be reciprocated.

The Daily Mail printed an article on 6th April 2016 about Jagger and The Stones by a well-known journalist, Toby Young, that, to me, was absolutely scathing. When I read it, I was furious that somebody could actually hold such a view. Of course, I understand that we all have our own opinions, and that they ought to be respected, but this one seemed to be too far way over the top. Just who was he pandering to?

Writing about the Stones Exhibitionism, he titled his article "From squalor to grasping cynicism: How rip-off tat for fans to buy, and recreated sixties bedsit, show that the new Rolling Stones show is nothing more than an exhibition in money making." The Rolling Stones Exhibition has attracted thousands of people in the various venues around the world. Young attacks Jagger's film career (based purely on *Ned Kelly*) their lack of a great record since *Some Girls* and he even proclaims that the tragedy of The Stones is that they didn't, unlike The Beatles, break up in 1970. His final dig is the age argument and he concludes "With a combined age of 286, isn't it about time they considered retirement?"

The article attracted 104 comments within the first few minutes and the hugely overwhelming majority did not side with the writer. Some did say that the merchandise at the venue was expensive and perhaps not brilliant BUT the history of the group was interesting to view and that Young was overlooking the musical excellence of the group. I am sure that the millions who saw the group from Glastonbury (2013) onwards to the end of the No Filter tour in the USA (2019 and 2021) would say just how good the group still are live and what a great show they had witnessed. Their partial return to form with a *Big Bang* in 2005 and the deservedly Grammy winning *Blue and Lonesome* album (2016) indicate that this group can still hold their heads up. Thank goodness they didn't do what The Beatles did in 1970 and just give up. Toby Young, you are well off the mark!

Enigma

Everything about Jagger is calculated. He is a very erudite person. *Sympathy For The Devil* bears this out well with probably his best writing. (See page 135).

Jagger's writing covers many topics and it is this diversity that I most enjoy. He is an enigma – a middle class background but purporting at times to be very working class. "You don't want my trousers to fall down, do you?" (shouted out between songs on the excellent, live, *Get Yer Ya-Yas Out* album).

If you listen to many of the interviews he has given over the years you will see that he has several voices. The quiet, earnest, upper class voice down to the cockney geezer. Those who choose to do impersonations always go to the latter. Jagger, since Glastonbury's triumphant set in 2013, seems to have gone from strength to strength. While people marvel at his physical fitness it is his voice that appears to be better now than ever.

It certainly became a little of a parody of itself from late 80s onwards, at times, as did his stage performance. Perhaps the video/song *Moves Like Jagger* by Maroon 5 helped him regain his former strengths or the fact that the band are playing better in more relaxed ways now. The intra-band squabbles of the past appear to be put to rest. Ronnie Wood appears to have a much more substantial role and, although he and Richards talk about the weaving of guitar parts, so they don't even know themselves who is playing what, there is no denying that his guitar work often drives the group on. The *Blue and Lonesome* CD, which I still play regularly, has given Jagger the opportunity to rediscover his blues voice which was always great. His harp playing too has never been better. The intensity is there again and the pleasure of singing is really evident. The recently released *Sticky Fingers Live at the Fonda Theatre* (2015) has a DVD performance which emphasises this return to form. Form which continued across the USA, South America, Cuba and the No Filter tour of Europe. They are undoubtedly still a tour de force.

Critics of the self-styled "Greatest Rock and Roll Band in the World" like to claim that The Stones have always been overshadowed by a rival - The Beatles in the 1960s, Queen in the 70s, U2 in the 80s, Coldplay in the noughties etc. But, to my mind, The Stones have outlasted them all, while remaining true to themselves as the prototype group for sex, drugs and rock and roll. The many hundreds of thousands who have seen them play in just the past five years will surely testify to this.

The first time I saw them: Hyde Park Concert 5 July 1969

I received quite a bit of censure from two or three of the older teaching colleagues at Duke of Bedford School, Thorney (one of the last two all age schools in the country with a 5 – 15 age range) when I announced in the staff room on the Friday afternoon what my plans for the weekend were. This was decadence incarnate as far as they were concerned. Mind you, if they had been there, they may well have found a lot of ammunition to fuel their theory. I went with my younger brother Paul, Brian

"Baggy" Alldread and another Stones fanatic, Dave Wilcocks. Baggy who died tragically young, used to keep us entertained with his 'Body Band'. He was nearly twenty years ahead of Bobby McFerrin of *Don't Worry, Be Happy* fame. He used various parts of his body to make different percussive sounds and the slightly moist armpit provided a loud squelching noise acting like a cymbal. I recall being reduced to tears when he played his version of "Satisfaction". Dave was probably a bigger fan of the Stones than me but was a serious young man and quite introspective. I was about five years older than the others so they looked up to me as if I knew what I was doing. I was dreading the underground as I could never work out which way the trains were headed but I need not have worried. The others seemed to know which way to go and I followed on.

We journeyed to Kings Cross from Peterborough station on a very sunny and warm day. Everything augured well for a huge outdoor concert - a free concert. I had been to nothing like it before and wondered what it would be like. At Kings Cross we took the underground to Hyde Park Corner on the Piccadilly Line. The carriage was full and there were a group of hippies sitting next to us. Four men and four women. They were almost indistinguishable by their dress with kaftans, headscarves sandals and beads and braided hair which was long and greasy. I felt certain that they were headed for the concert. But, no, they all stood up to get off a couple of stations before Hyde Park at Piccadilly Circus. Their leader – the one who had done all the talking – announced to his followers:

"Here, this is where we change!"

Having listened, fascinated by his talking non-stop throughout the journey, I could not prevent myself from remarking quite loudly:

"Oh! What into?"

He looked me straight in the eye and answered without hesitation:

"Pumpkins, silly boy. Pumpkins". He accentuated the second 'pumpkins' with an outstretched arm and a finger pointed right at me in true Lord Kitchener style. With that he turned and alighted from the carriage onto the platform with his entourage in tow. Of course I have many memories of the actual concert, and the array of different bands that I hadn't really heard much of before, but pumpkins always come to mind. I often wonder what he is doing now - probably a retired accountant.

The concert coincided with the death of Brian Jones who had been dismissed from the group in June, and had died in suspicious circumstances just days before the Hyde Park concert. This would be the very first time that Mick Taylor publicly performed with the group.

I have always had some time for Jagger as an actor, *Ned Kelly* and its atrocious Irish accent notwithstanding, but, noble though the sentiments were, in Shelley's elegy that he quoted to lament Brian's passing, it did sound rather incongruous, awkward and slightly misplaced. It must have been a difficult thing to do. Jones had been ejected from the group some little time before because he had become a passenger and was wasted a lot of the time. Two days before this, already arranged, concert, he died. Something had to be said and it most certainly was not the place for recriminations. A conciliatory tone had to be adopted and the archaic phrasing of Shelley's words did have an element of gravitas, if nothing else.

The Stones were always a raw band, particularly in their early days, and that aptly summed up their performance during this concert. Viewing the video *Stones in the Park* (and later the DVD version) to recapture those moments, it is very difficult to say that it was one of their best performances. Where we were, seated on the ground, very far back, we could not see that the butterflies that Jagger released after reading the elegy, had been kept cooped up so long that many of them fluttered to the ground upon being released. Granada TV filmed the concert and I remember hardly being able to wait until it was broadcast. Of course you look to see if you are captured on film with the audience shots. We were not. I was able to see in close up what I had only really heard. The crowd was reported at the time as being a quarter of a million, but it actually seemed a lot more. There were bodies as far as the eye could see both on the ground and, for some people, up in the trees. There was a public systems announcement – among the many that were made that day, that I always remember. As I have just said there were many people up in the trees. The announcer made a very 'love and peace' plea to them. He stated that there must 300 people in that tree (without saying which tree) and that they should show respect for the tree. Needless to say, I saw nobody actually coming down from any of the trees.

The whole day was amazing. The giant three- and four-day concerts and festivals that proliferate the summer seasons nowadays, with their sprawling masses, were scarcely known then. The legendary Woodstock

Festival was due to take place the following month in New York State. This epoch changing event in the history of Rock music would change peoples' perceptions forever. The "half a million strong" to quote Joni Mitchell's song, would print an indelible mark on all future festivals of this kind. The huge sea of people at the Hyde Park concert was an important precursor to all of this though we didn't know it at the time. I knew the group Family (with Roger Chapman's uniquely distinctive voice) and the Third Ear Band - I had always listened to John Peel who championed groups like that– but I did not know King Crimson. Their first record, *In the Court of the Crimson King,* which formed the basis of their set, was, and still remains, a favourite album of mine. Being far back from the stage area, the gentle wind sometimes caused the sound to swirl, making their music even more ethereal and haunting. *Twenty First Century Schizoid Man,* with its snarling climax, sounded incredible though I did not know its title till I bought the album later.

I mentioned earlier that I have never smoked a cigarette in my life, but I know that, passively, I must have inhaled a lot of the sweet-smelling smoke that day that many in the crowd seemed to be enjoying. Rather like attending one of those annual Eric Clapton concerts at the Royal Albert Hall, the atmosphere was ripe with substance smoke.

I quoted the "pumpkins incident" earlier: I have another 'P' word memory of that day. We had, as I said, travelled down on the day but thousands must have camped overnight. We had to step over large numbers of people still in their sleeping bags like a sea of multi- coloured cocoons stretched out in front of us. As we made our way further into the park, past the sleeping bag army, traipsing through the throngs of people on the grass (no pun intended) I espied this woman who was doing a swirling, dervish dance round and round. Her very flimsy skirt was flying around with her and I couldn't help noticing that her bikini briefs were a very vivid shade of purple. As we got much closer the image became clearer. She was not actually wearing any underwear at all, but had dyed her pubic hair purple. This was eye opening stuff even for a 22-year-old in 1969.

We also walked past a rather stunning looking woman with a see-through blouse and a large Afro hairstyle. I didn't give her any more thought until I was watching a music programme on TV -possibly Top of the Pops – a year or so later. Who should be singing *Walk On Gilded Splinters*? Yes, the woman with the see-through blouse. It was Marsha Hunt, who in November 2012 had to sell her love letter correspondence with Mick Jagger (the father of her only child – his first) in order to help pay for the upkeep of her house. This time she was wearing something similarly outrageous - a very short top that covered the top half of her breasts and left the underside exposed.

I also recall seeing a number of men in German army helmets and Nazi regalia wandering around as we got there. Even to a young History teacher, with a 20th Century specialist background, this looked rather odd. It was not, however, till I saw the ITV screening of the show, that I found out that they were some form of Hells Angel security group for the concert. Fortunately, they were blessed with a lot more luck than their American counterparts were to have at Altamont later that year.

ST⬤NES MISCELLANY #2

Hyde Park Set list:
I'm Yours and I'm Hers
Jumpin' Jack Flash
Mercy Mercy Down Home Girl
Stray Cat Blues
No Expectations I'm Free
Loving Cup
Love in Vain
(I Can't Get No) Satisfaction
Honky Tonk Women
Midnight Rambler
Street Fighting Man
Sympathy for the Devil

I certainly did not recognise the opening number which I discovered later was a Johnny Winter song. He has been known for a number of Rolling Stones cover versions (you must check out his rip-roaring version of *Jumping Jack Flash)* so it seemed apt. I also did not know one or two of their own songs and, again found out later that this would be the first time that they had been performed. The guy introducing them heralded the group as "the greatest Rock 'n' Roll band in the world". In my eyes, by 1969, they were just that. Apparently, this same epithet was used on the ensuing American tour and Jagger is reputed to have disliked it. Whatever the case, those words have been uttered very many times since. Justifiably, too, in my humble opinion.

Though some critics, who love to point to their age, make zimmer frame references and the like, have questioned their standing in the Pantheon of Rock, in my eyes, each time I have seen them they have produced a better show. I have seen B.B. King several times and went to one of his farewell tour concerts in the UK (NEC, Birmingham with Gary Moore supporting in 2006) and nobody questioned the fact that at his age - he was born in 1925 - he played virtually all the time seated on a chair or stool. John Lee Hooker, another favourite, was a similar case. I saw Dave 'Honeyboy' Edwards at the Boat House in Cambridge when he was approaching his nineties. He actually knew and played with the famed pioneer of the blues - Robert Johnson. The Stones have recorded and played a number of Johnson's songs. Age then, is not, nor never should be, the criteria by which musicians are judged. I have always had a wide, catholic taste in music and to me there are only two types: good music and bad music. You either like it or you don't. It is what the music conveys to you that is all important.

During The Stones' set the audience appreciation was lifted greatly. It was this group that they had come to see despite the plethora of talent among the supporting artists. Some of the fans were clearly high on something – and not just up a tree. I doubt whether it was just the excitement of seeing their heroes but a number of mostly shirtless, long haired, men stood up to do what was to become a familiar sight at most ensuing concerts with their version of a free dance. I don't know if it has a particular name, but it involved shutting your eyes, shaking your head fiercely, though not the full head banging you get at Heavy Metal concerts and waving your arms about frenziedly sometimes in unison with the music. Each 'dancer' seemed to have his (it was almost always a man) own particular version of the manoeuvre. It was always entertaining; dare I say amusing?

45

In retrospect this concert was to have a major influence on my concert going and my admiration for the Stones. Yes, the performance was a little patchy. I recall that *Midnight Rambler* (a song I hadn't heard before) was a stand-out performance as was *Sympathy For The Devil*, the number they closed with. It took a little time to get going and for everyone to be in sync with everyone else in the band but a very powerful song indeed. The band of African musicians who provided the basic samba drumbeat played for quite a few minutes before the song finally kicked in. It was almost as if they were getting warmed up before the song could commence. As I have discovered, in the ensuing years, Stones' concerts had very little to do with ultra clean, professional musicianship, but always the power, intensity and integrity of performance. This rawness added to the overall performance. In this instance, however, partly because of the timing of Brian's death and the rapid introduction of Mick Taylor, the event itself became greater than the actual performance.

In 1971, in an interview with *Rolling Stone* magazine, Keith Richards said, "We played pretty bad until near the end, because we hadn't played for years... Nobody minded, because they just wanted to hear us play again". This was the first time since the European Tour of 1967 that they had played in public. With the sacking of Jones there had been little real time for rehearsal for Mick Taylor who must have been very nervous.

The fascinating footnote to this concert is, that while writing this section of the account, the Stones announced that they would play Hyde Park in 2013 almost 44 years to the day - this time on Saturday 6th July. I couldn't get a ticket, despite frantic dialling (more difficult from

Greece), as the event sold out within three minutes - testament to their drawing power indeed. Guess what? They only bloody announced a second Hyde Park gig and I didn't notice in time. Do people really care about the high prices of the tickets? Apparently the event is one not to be missed whatever the price. The O2 concerts (2012) attracted the same press criticism regarding cost but were similarly sold out. People will pay to see quality and with The Rolling Stones that is virtually guaranteed. I like Bob Dylan but you can never tell what sort of performance he is likely to produce. I suspect that even he doesn't really know either nor perhaps even care. I have a friend who is a major Dylan fan and he bought five tickets for a series of shows stating that he knew Bob would be good at, at least, one of them. I have seen Dylan only twice – once, the whole thing was magnificent, the second far less so. You do not get this inconsistency with The Stones. You can rely on the group to perform at their utmost and almost always a solid, good two-hour set.

In retrospect I did buy the DVD of this later concert. The performance is so much more polished than the first Hyde Park outing which is partly due to the much-advanced technical side of the filming. The enjoyment of the group is instantly visible. The 1969 version, however, is more important for the reasons I gave earlier and remains a socially significant event from the sixties.

TV Infamy
1967 had been the last time The Stones had performed their European Tour and one which was punctuated with riots in a number of cities on the Continent. There was a chance to see them on TV that year, however. I was really pleased to see that they were scheduled to play the top-

ranking entertainment TV show – Sunday Night At The London Palladium – a show I rarely watched.

One week before this performance they had played the Ed Sullivan Show in the USA on the 15th of January, just after the release of *Between The Buttons*, their latest album. They were forced to change the lyrics to the A-side of their single *Let's Spend The Night Together* to "some time" together so as not to offend the delicate sensibilities of the American TV viewers.

In the weeks that followed The Stones had the word "night" bleeped out of that record and some stations went as far as banning it all together, which meant *Ruby Tuesday* (the B-side) got a lot more airplay, with the result that it topped the charts, while *Let's Spend The Night Together* could only make a lowly No.55 in the US charts.

In Britain, having frequently been asked to appear, and never doing so, they had relented, yet no one from The Stones can quite remember why, and decided to appear on Sunday Night At The London Palladium. On the TV show, The Stones mimed, while Mick sang live to *Ruby Tuesday, Let's Spend The Night Together*, and *Connection* - the latter being a track from the newly released *Between The Buttons* album. One reason for their appearance was that opportunities to appear on TV had decreased as *Ready Steady Go!*, the best of the 1960's pop programmes, had been just very recently taken off the air; it was also true that Sunday Night At The London Palladium had a huge audience, close to 10 million. Miming was rife on British TV, but you could see that Jagger was singing live.

It was not the miming that was controversial and caused a big issue in the press; it was that The Stones refusal to appear on the closing sequence of the TV show. They refused to stand on the stage, when all the performers and the show's host, Dave Allen, were expected to smile and wave to the audience as the carousel revolved. Andrew Loog Oldham apparently had a row with Mick about it, and, in the following days, many angry viewers took to writing letters to the press. This was just "not on"!

The row seemed to go on for weeks after. Those of a certain age couldn't comprehend why The Stones had been invited to appear in the first place. Younger people couldn't care less, and some others probably felt like The Stones – why, then, did they appear? One of the big features of the show was this revolving stage at the end where all the acts that had appeared waved inanely at the audience in the theatre and at home. The refusal to go round and round may have been because "the joint wasn't rocking!!"

Personally, I liked the fact that they had chosen not to conform and was surprised at the outcry in the press. I am quite certain that the real reason they decided to appear on the show was to help plug the new album. The controversy would certainly keep them, and the newly released record, in the limelight. Apparently, the following week, the show starred Peter Cook and Dudley Moore, who were friends of The Stones. To show their solidarity with Mick, Keith and the boys, they went on the roundabout with life size cardboard cut outs of all five Stones, created by Gerald Scarfe. I only heard about this afterwards, not having watched the show but dearly wished that I had.

The Beatles, who had appeared in 1963 at The Palladium, had done the carousel thing. 'Nuff said.

Relevance and Music Style

Before I get onto the age old question Beatles or The Stones I want to say a few words about the relevance of Mick and the boys. I have always had a good sense of humour but never taken to those who just pick on the combined ages and dismiss the group as if this was a fault or hindrance. Sloppy, lazy journalism is to blame here. I similarly have never liked the Freddy Starr style mimicry of Jagger's moves seriously either. It ceases to be funny and becomes boring. To me The Rolling Stones have always been of their time whenever it is.

There is no doubt that the string of albums in the late 60s to the mid 70's was phenomenal but that does not automatically mean that they are past their sell by date now. The fact that people of all ages turn out to see them all over the world in massive numbers bears testimony to that. The million plus audience at Copacabana Beach in Brazil and the half a million in the recent Cuba concert are the two best examples. When you also take in the fact that these audiences were ecstatic and singing along to the well-known songs emphasizes this relevance. The fact that these were free concerts is irrelevant here. The fans knew the words and were genuinely happy to be there. They were true fans.

Something else I like is that Jagger usually says a few words in the language of the country that the concert is taking place. Not a typical Brit then! His Spanish would have come with his time with Bianca and his French from his time as a tax exile in the South of France - would you pay the 93% tax as imposed by Harold Wilson's Labour Government?

The Stones regularly appear either at the top or close to it in the ratings for concert goers and revenues every time that they hit the road has to count for something. Their album *Blue and Lonesome* which has global sales, at the time of writing, in excess of three million, also won a Grammy for Best Traditional Blues Album in 2018. The appeal is still there and, again, at time of writing, we await the first studio album of original songs with great anticipation, I would also like to see another blues covers album as they do it so well. The track written during Covid lockdown -*Living In A Ghost Town* -actually topped the iTunes download charts in 2020 again adding credence to their relevance. (See Page 180)

How can you not like Jagger, whose love life has been microscopically scrutinized, when he comes up with a self-deprecating lyric like 'Once upon a time I was your little rooster, but am I just one of your cocks?' from *Rough Justice* in 2005 on the *Bigger Bang* album To be a touch more serious, the lyrics of a great number of his songs are outstandingly written. There will be a specific and more detailed reference to this in the section on my favourite Rolling Stones tracks.

Many groups from the sixties have long disappeared or turn up with one or no original members at holiday camp weekends still plying their trade. They have become parodies of themselves. Some, I hasten to mention, were almost parodies when they started. The Stones, despite those who like to say that they should give up now – zimmer frame jokes to the fore – have never been parodies. They play their old catalogue certainly but with gusto and freshness. They are not playing at it but still believe in what they do and enjoy the moment. Their sets last two hours or so and despite Charlie's[1] occasional murmurings about packing up, it seems that they, like many of their blues heroes, will go on till they drop.

The political commentator Adam Boulton, on Sky News in 2018 when The Stones were playing their excellently received tour of the UK, remarked, and I wrote it down at that time, noting that "The Stones are different. They are still a contemporary phenomenon as demonstrated by the scale, expense and popularity of their tour." I could not agree more. I did find it slightly incongruous that Adam Boulton, staid political commentator, would utter such praise. He is one of the people I would least expect to make such a comment. Perhaps someone else penned it for him. Perhaps he really is a fan. The old Blues song *You Can't Judge A Book By Looking At The Cover* springs to mind.

There are those critics of The Stones who say that there music is very predictable. You can transpose the opening riff from any song and follow it with any other song and it all sounds the same. These, in my eyes, are from the Mary Whitehouse School of Criticism: very often condemning something without having seen or heard it.

The music of The Stones is very wide in content and style which might surprise those who have chosen not to listen to the albums and dismissed the group as one trick ponies. Blues features, of course, *(Love in Vain, Ventilator Blues, Ride 'em On Down)*, Rock certainly *(Jumpin' Jack Flash, Satisfaction, Street Fighting Man)* Soul *(Ain't Too Proud To Beg, Harlem Shuffle, Just My Imagination)*, Disco *(Miss You, If I Were A Dancer part 2,*

---

[1] See the special tribute to Charlie (page 244)

Emotional Rescue) but also reggae (*Cherry Oh Baby, Hey Negrita, Send It To Me)* and some great Country and Western (*Far Away Eyes, Dead Flowers, Sweet Virginia")* and even soft ballads (*Angie, Wild Horses, Winter)* Punk (*Respectable, Where The Boys Go, She's So Cold)* I liked it all. There are political songs like *Under cover of the Night, We Love You, Sweet Neo Con* and even tongue in cheek parodies ("I drove twenty red lights in his honour. Thank you, Jesus. Thank you Lord" from *Faraway Eyes)*.

Like many, I didn't particularly revere their *Satanic Majesties* album at that time, in its bid to join the Sgt. Pepper psychedelic train. It DID, however, contain some memorable songs like *She's A Rainbow, 2000 Light Years From Home* and "*Citadel.* The album has undergone a recent reappraisal and is not quite so widely disliked. *Satanic Majesties* also boasts a track written and credited to Bill Wyman –*In Another Land*, which was released as a single and was a small hit in the USA. It reached Number 87 on the Billboard charts. Another Stones album which often fails to attract much support is *Dirty Work* but I find the track and accompanying video for *One Hit To The Body* really solid and extremely amusing as it was recorded at the height of the Jagger Richards falling out from 1986. The thrusting and aggressive moves by both Jagger and Richards on the video show real menace especially from Richards. Is he going to hit him?

The examples that I cite here bear testimony to the fact that The Rolling Stones cover a very wide range of music genres and help to reinforce the point I made about their relevance.

John Lennon, just after The Beatles had disintegrated, in an interview with David Wigg in 1971, claimed: "For me personally when you listen to The Stones music, nothing's ever happened. It's the same old stuff goes on and on and on. I've never heard anything different from them. So I think it would be good if they broke up and made some individual music because it's the same old hash, rehash of the same old stuff over and over again."

As I have demonstrated above, especially at the time of that run of four masterful albums, this view is so misguided. There is a world of different music genres to be discovered. Of course Lennon is entitled to his view as, indeed, I am. He has totally misrepresented his biggest rivals. He did, however, like to stir things up in controversial ways himself. He courted controversy. Was he bigger than Jesus?

In order to emphasize this point further I want to draw your attention to Pitchfork.com (an American online music magazine) who provide a very interesting article on the best Rolling Stones songs that don't really sound like The Rolling Stones which I have included as an appendix (see Appendix C page 215)

The Beatles or The Rolling Stones?
I cannot put off The Beatles or The Stones argument any longer. Nearly sixty years on the debate is still active for some fans.

The introspective artistes vs. the bad boys. Tom Wolfe is reputed to have said "The Beatles want to hold your hand, but The Stones want to burn down your town." My take on this would be to use respective song titles. The Beatles wanted to *Hold Your Hand* while the Stones

Wanna Make Love To You or *Spend The Night Together*. The distinction may not sound much but, in the context of the day, it was clear enough. The latter song was even causing problems as late as 2006 when The Stones provided the half time "entertainment" at Super Bowl XL. Yet again for American TV they had to sing "spend SOME TIME together" in case it disturbed the sensibilities of particularly the Bible Belt. After the nipple, or wardrobe malfunction, incident of Janet Jackson at a previous Super Bowl show, the TV executives had to be very wary. I have referred earlier to their 1967 appearance on the Ed Sullivan Show where the same censorship had happened. Were The Stones really still seen as a possible risk forty four years into their career? Rebels for all of their lives? Come on - to use their first single title – be serious.

If you were a child of the sixties, it had to be The Beatles or The Stones – not The Beatles AND The Stones. For many of us, the "rivalry" was clearly defined though it was actually more imagined than real — The Beatles and Stones were friends though probably not that close. They even used to contact each other before a single was to be released so that they were not released on the same day. This ensured they would both have the chance for a Number One record.

It was an existential "either/or" question. It came down to personal choice, obviously, and self-perceived identity. Certainly in my circle of friends, almost exclusively from the same all boys Grammar school, there was no question. It was The Rolling Stones for us. At parties the first two Stones' LPs almost always provided the backdrop to a successful event. I would never go as far as to say The Beatles were for girls and The Stones were for boys but at that time that is how I perceived it. I did come to respect some of The Beatles music later but nothing before *Day Tripper* really excited me. With my disparaging comments about Paul McCartney I had to check to see who had written *Day Tripper*. It was John Lennon. I have to admit buying the first Beatles LP – mainly because it was the thing to do; everyone had it – but I then swapped it, with a school friend, for the Del Shannon LP *Hats Off To Larry* which I played to death, especially the up tempo track *So Long Baby*. This was for me a much more exciting record than The Beatles *Please, Please Me* album. I realise that I would be in a minority to think in such a way but that is how I felt. I had heard a previous LP the group had put out with Tony Sheridan and to me this was like a Music Hall record with too many standard, old fashioned, songs. (*My Bonnie Lies Over The Ocean,* for goodness sake or *Octopus's Garden* later on.) I could never imagine The Stones making such a record even when they were just performing cover versions. They had more taste.

I think one of the things that turned me off The Beatles was their success. I found the group's overwhelming popularity and commercialization alienating. Their show bizzy glitz was a turn off for me. I could never really like a group that even my grandmother liked. There was too much media adulation. I needed someone more in keeping with what I believed in. I refused to be caught up in the Beatlemania crowd like some of my classmates. Part of my teenage rebellion, certainly not atypical, was trying to be different. I never smoked a cigarette at the back (or the front for that matter) of the bike sheds at school or anywhere else. My parents always supported Cambridge in the Boat Race because we lived near Cambridge. I plumped for Oxford. Not really earth shattering rebellion then. For me, then, it was The Rolling Stones, The Pretty Things (who did actually have Dick Taylor who had briefly been a Rolling Stone) and Them (with the wonderful Van Morrison fronting the group). My parents' generation, and elements of the media, did not seem to be on the right wavelength. My dad liked The Bachelors with *I Believe* (he used to sing the line "I believe for every drop of rain that falls, someone gets wet" which was quite amusing the first time, at least), Billy J Kramer and The Dakotas and particularly their recording of *Little Children* and Herman's Hermits with *No Milk Today...* say no more! That was their problem. I became hooked by The Stones' blues rock-based "harder" sound. As I could see it, how could you not be hooked by the riffs of *Satisfaction, Paint It Black"* and *Jumping Jack Flash* - still absolute classics rather than the asinine, slushy offerings favoured by my dad? His favourite film was *"South Pacific"*.

I have never liked Paul McCartney. He was always too pretty and twee for me. My sister and her friends liked him. Some of the Beatles output that has his hand on it, like *"Yesterday, Long & Winding Road* and *Hey Jude,* I just cannot abide. *Hey Jude*'s ending just goes on and on and on, and, if I haven't already switched it off, or changed radio stations, it makes me feel ill. I did like the attitude and swagger of John Lennon however, who, for me, was much more in keeping with the image The Stones projected. It was Lennon who sneeringly described some of McCartney's songs as "granny music shit" according to engineer Geoff Emerick. Asked who wrote *When I'm Sixty Four* in his 1980 talk with

'Playboy', Lennon said it was Paul's completely. "I would never write a song like that".

Pete Townsend, who I rate highly, said in 1982 "To me, rock was The Rolling Stones, and before that, Chuck Berry, but I can't really include The Beatles in that. The Beatles were over with Herman's Hermits. That's not rock & roll." He went on to wonder why Americans always thought of the Fab Four as rock when "they were such a big pop phenomenon." As to Beatles songs he did enjoy, Townshend saw it as "light music with occasional masterpieces thrown in." I have to say that this verdict is very much in line with my own. Michael Stipe of R.E.M famously regarded The Beatles' songs as elevator music. Rather mischieviously, Stipe preferred *Yummy,Yummy, Yummy* by the Ohio Express.. They were leading exponents of what was deemed Bubblegum music themselves.

The reality was that The Beatles and The Rolling Stones did actually get on well with each other but it served them to have this faux rivalry openly aired. The Beatles performed *All You Need Is Love* in the world's first live, international, satellite television production "Our World", which was broadcast around the world on 25 June 1967. They invited many of their friends to the event to create a festive atmosphere and to join in on the song's chorus. Among the friends were members of The Rolling Stones, Eric Clapton and Marianne Faithfull. I remember seeing Mick Jagger and Keith sitting cross legged "in the crowd".

A small confession. I did buy the *Sgt Pepper* LP (mono version) and still have the cardboard cut-out bits that came within the sleeve. This was for some form of investment. *Rolling Stone Magazine's* 2012 edition of the 500 Greatest Albums is a book I cherish and tick off any album that I have that is in it – which number well over half of the 500 albums. From the Top Ten listed in the book I have *Sgt Pepper* plus six other albums including *Exile On Main Street* by you know who. There are two other Beatles records in the top ten but I do not have those. My reason for keeping *Sgt Pepper* is that as an historian and one who is immersed in music, I felt I ought to have a copy even though I do not play it. The Stones have ten albums in this top 500. My son, Christian, when I was sixty-four, made a pastiche of this iconic cover as a birthday card with four pictures of me as the four Beatles. We do still speak to each other!

A relatively recently released song featuring Lennon with Mick Jagger on a song called *Too Many Cooks* demonstrates that there had to have been some sort of co-operation, if not, friendship. It was recorded in 1973 and, after being "rediscovered", added to *The Very Best Of Mick Jagger* CD that was released in 2007.

I cannot deny the fact that the second single released by The Rolling Stones was the Lennon/McCartney penned *I Wanna Be Your Man* recorded separately by The Beatles (with Ringo on vocals) and The Rolling Stones. The Stones' version was released a few weeks earlier. The song was finished by John and Paul in the corner of a room while Mick Jagger and Keith Richards looked on. There are various accounts of how this came about but the most common is that the two Beatles bumped into the Stones on the street. They booked into a recording session at De Lane Lea Studio and completed a song that had already been worked on. The Stones' version is a frenetic electric rock/blues song featuring Brian Jones' distinctive slide guitar and Bill Wyman's driving bass playing - a much superior version to The Beatles one.

There have been very many online polls which ask you to decide which is the best group and The Beatles/Stones question is ever *present. project Malamute on Friday February 15th, 2013 stated: I'll put forth the notion that not only did The Beatles write better songs and make better albums, they were a better live band. I'll even contend that they 'rocked' more. If by 'rocked' you mean came out and delivered a tight, powerful, no frills, performance. Mick Jagger couldn't sing like either of these guys, and The Stones were a sloppy, half assed, phone-it-in-because-I'd-rather-be-off-shooting-heroin live band in comparison.*

This is a typical pro-Beatle argument that I could, and would, never agree with. The Beatles were NEVER seriously regarded as a great live band. Perhaps the tone deaf felt this way. Those early shots of them in the USA at Shea Stadium, for example, where they couldn't even hear themselves, looks powerful and raw but in reality they might not even have bothered to play anything. They could have mimed. The Beatles were a studio band. They were a Pop Music band. George Martin's musical influence is legendary and it is difficult to argue against the production values on *Revolver* and *Sgt Pepper* but for real power and rawness, it will always be The Stones for me. Under the heavy guidance of George Martin, The Beatles represented the old Tin Pan Alley populism albeit wrapped in their master's strings, woodwind and piano based melodies. They created their own blueprint for mainstream pop at which they admittedly had few, if any, equals.

For me The Rolling Stones stayed true to their R'n'B roots by utilising the raw elements of the music from the other side of the Atlantic and developing as they went along. Especially as they traversed the USA, in those early days, they accumulated new sounds and styles that they were able to transmit via their four successive career defining albums - *"Beggars Banquet ('68), Let It Bleed ('69), Sticky Fingers ('71)* and *"Exile On Main Street" ('72).*

I loved -and still do - their belligerent attitude and swagger. Their blues roots developed into what we now recognise as Rock. The four albums mentioned above surely meant that the epithet "The Greatest Rock n Roll Band in the world" was justified and they have lived up to this to this day. The excellent Tom Petty recalled to CBC in 2014 "They were my punk music, They were grittier than The Beatles it was rawer. They played blues in this really energetic kind of raw way, but it wasn't complicated."

The Beatles played together, live, for the last time in January 1969 on the roof of the Apple Records building in London. For me they had already started to lose their edge. Their last proper tour was actually in 1966. The dynamics within the group appear to have been shaken by Yoko Ono's involvement. The group was visibly imploding. The internal divisions between all four of the now not quite so "Fab Four" became really serious and I doubt if the feud between Mick and Keith was ever so acrimonious but then I would think that, wouldn't I?

The ability to play live and to more than just replicate their records is a virtue indeed. The Rolling Stones and their concerts have always been events with a capital "E", and on an increasingly grander scale, as time progressed. The impact of such events is almost immeasurably great. The Hyde Park Concert in '69, as an example, was a huge media extravaganza as well as one of the archetypal events of the sixties. The Stones' performance on the day is almost incidental yet still a defining moment of the era.

Jagger, as a front man and singer, is the real deal. Be it blues, rock, country, reggae; be it ballad or rocker, he has it all. Justin Hayward once sang "I'm just a singer in a rock and roll band": for me, there is only one singer in a rock n roll band and no "just" about it – Mick Jagger. He has been described in the press as all hips and lips but to me he is much more than that – a true musician through and through.

I know this is all subjective – rather like the judging at gymnastics or high board diving – but if we take the classic Barrett Strong track *Money (that's What I Want)*, a great Motown song in its own right, and then compare the versions offered by both the emerging British groups, for me the case is proved. The song was a staple number in the repertoire of many up-and-coming bands back in those days before writing your own material was considered as essential. Lennon's vocal on the song from their second LP is certainly raw and the piano part is very faithful to the original, but it takes the Jagger led version (from their first EP) solidly driven by Bill Wyman's bass guitar to make the superior cover version. Even though The Stones' version has a rather poppy, repeated "that's what I want", it still has the edge. The dirty sound of the guitars, the harmonica and use of echo, set the mood magnificently - a truly R 'n' B experience.

Jagger's recent heart surgery in 2019 has seen him return to the USA on the "No Filter" tour. His performances have been very highly acclaimed, and the band has seen a drink free Ronnie Wood playing the best he ever has. I saw The Stones in Manchester in 2018 and was amazed at just how good they still are (See the concert review later in the book page 170). Jagger re-found his voice on the *Blue and Lonesome* album and this has carried on into some of his best performances for many years.

The strength of the keyboard players they have had over the years is another powerful dimension, too. Poor old Ian 'Stu' Stewart (not permitted by Loog Oldham to be an official member of the group as he looked too ordinary), Nicky Hopkins and now Chuck Leavell have all had significant roles to play and feature on some of the very best Stones' tracks. As a live band they have always been supreme in my eyes with their concert performances regularly overshadowing the studio recordings. Very few groups have been able to say that and sustain it especially over such a long period of time.

In an excerpt from *Play It Loud!* - a book for guitar aficionados, authors Brad Tolinski and Alan di Perna state: "To young rock and roll audience at the time, The Rolling Stones offered a kind of primal, dark, Dionysiac alternative to The Beatles' more sunny, well groomed Apollonian appeal" Another author, Steven Hyden (Your Favorite Band Is Killing Me: What Pop Music Rivalries Reveal About the Meaning of Life) argues that loving The Rolling Stones is synonymous with cool, while The Beatles are ordinary in comparison.

Stones versus Beatles – a rivalry, Hyden insists, that's really about the Beatles' cultural hegemony. "Loving The Beatles is so ordinary by comparison," he writes. "It says nothing about you other than your unquestioning acceptance of inevitable truths."

I loved it in 1965 when The Beach Boys won the accolade as the world's best group displacing the Beatles. I have always admired Brian Wilson especially when I found that he was stone deaf in one ear after being mistreated by his father. My pleasure was that the dominance that The Beatles seemed to have been broken. They were not invincible. I still loved The Stones - the best group for me. The Beatles, as I stated earlier, owed a great deal to George Martin. I could never say that they were not a good group nor that I didn't like some of their music but many of the McCartney songs I do dislike. *Hey Jude* is the example I keep repeating. I loved the Wilson Pickett version but then the classic *In The Midnight Hour* singer had a really great voice.

In 1966 it was also decreed (at least by the NME Poll Winners Charts) that The Beach Boys were the best group in the world. I would have placed The Stones at number one with The Beach Boys second, but had no major qualms with the result. The autobiography *I am Brian Wilson* co-written with Ben Greenman in 2016, makes a surprising revelation about The Rolling Stones. It is fairly common knowledge that McCartney is a huge Beach Boys fan and that Brian regarded The Beatles as huge rivals especially after the *Sgt Pepper* album was released. I was at the Royal Festival Hall when Brian, with the excellent Wondermints providing the backing, recreated the exceptional *Pet Sounds* in 2002. McCartney was in the audience and acknowledged from the stage by Wilson. Everybody got up and whooped and cheered when it was announced. I say everybody. I, rather childishly, remained glued to my seat.

In this autobiography Wilson reveals that he was also obsessed by The Rolling Stones. The Beach Boys *Add Some Music To Your Day* was, in Wilson's words "an attempt to corral the Stones' vibe... Our voices are like the Stones' guitars". Wilson is widely regarded as a musical genius and who am I to disregard his choice here?

I hesitate to mention Ringo's vocal efforts here either. Pure vaudeville. I always loved John Lennon's reply to a question about Ringo's contribution to the band when he claimed, probably jokingly, that Ringo wasn't even the best drummer in the group. Ringo was probably more akin to The Monkees than The Beatles. I have never regarded him as a serious musician. An entertainer – possibly. He always had an amusing ready retort.

I cannot think of any Stones song that I could not bear to listen to even though it might not be one of their many classic renditions. I do not subscribe to the view that they lost their creativity in the late 70s and haven't written anything good since. People form these opinions and then seek to fulfill them by shutting their minds as well as their ears.

As I was proof reading this book I happened upon an article from The Sunday Post (23rd September 2019) a weekly Scottish newspaper, which had the following title: "Author Ian Rankin hails anniversary of Rolling Stones' classic album and reveals why his famous detective Rebus could never be a Beatles fan" He recounts how *Let It Bleed*, which is getting a 50 year revamp, has been bought by him five times over in different formats and how it is his very favourite record. He based his famous detective Rebus on Ian Stewart who also came from Fife He has named some of his books after Stones' titles. He writes "When I started writing about Rebus, I knew that he would be a big fan, a fan of that earthy, bluesy nature of The Stones compared to the Beatles. The Stones were seen as the mavericks, the outsiders and the bad boys, of being dangerous in a way the Beatles were not". When *Let It Bleed* was released it was at a time when the hippie, flowers in your hair, era was coming to a shattering halt with the ill-fated Altamont Festival and the embarrassing failings in the Viet Nam war. Rankin loves the blues in the album and remarks that the blues are often dark and about "murder and mayhem".

He makes a very interesting point, which probably is coincidental rather than prophetic, about the back cover of the album. Most people probably don't know that a then, largely undiscovered Delia Smith, baked the cake for the front cover. The back cover shows the cake broken up with the record underneath smashed up and in pieces. An allegory for the times? Probably not. I have to admit I had never made that connection but it does serve to hasten the collapse of hippiedom even if coincidental. I have always been a big fan of the Rebus books and have the DVD set with both John Hannah and Ken Stott as the lead character. It was really good to get a very strong endorsement for The Stones over The Beatles from such an eminent source.

In October 2021 "McCartney disses the Rolling Stones" was the headline in *USA Today* and an array of newspapers round the world. This verdict from Sir Paul came ahead of McCartney's "The Lyrics: 1956 to the Present," a book from Nov. 2nd, 2021 which collected the lyrics of 154 of his songs including *Eleanor Rigby* and *Band on the Run* and the release of *The Beatles: Get Back,* a documentary series directed by Peter Jackson, and screened in November 2021 on Disney+. McCartney claimed the Stones were just a blues cover band – nothing more. He had put the Stones down the previous year, too, on the Howard Stern Show. Jagger's response was "The Rolling Stones is a big concert band when the Beatles never even did an arena tour. That's the real big difference between these two bands. One band is unbelievably luckily still playing in stadiums, and then the other band doesn't exist." Macca's 2021 words surely used to stir up the press and help publicise his forthcoming projects. It's not as if he needs the money! He is the one who is raking up the past. How insecure is that?

School times: NME story

I have to apologise to poor old NAJ (Mr Johnson, I am sorry) We all - Dave Bishop, Keith Lines, Wiggy (Brian Smith) and I - used to get NME on a Friday morning, We all lived in the same area and often used to meet in the newsagents on the corner of Newark Avenue on a Friday morning en route to school which was quite close by. We used to have NAJ first thing that day in our 5th Year, and took it to read during his English lessons at that time. The NME often had The Stones featured on the front cover. During our lesson with NAJ, one of us would have the double paged paper open wide whenever he turned round or glanced up. Of course he confiscated it. A few minutes later someone else would do the same and so on. This spread through other members of the class in succeeding weeks. I think NAJ used to expect it. We always got them back at the end of the lesson though. I think he got his own back a year or so later when I wanted to train with the school rowing team (which he ran) because I was turned down. Never made me bitter though!! When studying English at A level, he was one of the three teachers we had and I found what a really nice guy he was and felt a bit ashamed even at the time. He should have kept the NMEs. I wish I had. It would have provided some excellent source material for something like this!

Christmas Party

As a teacher: I taught at Stanground College in Peterborough for very many years and always enjoyed the end of term activities. One year during the mid-1970s we held our Staff Christmas party at the Great Northern Hotel just across from Peterborough Railway North Station. It stands out in my memory for two reasons. We always had had a good meal – traditional fare and then the disco. I always used to ask the DJ for *Brown Sugar* from *Sticky Fingers* at this sort of event otherwise I might not be tempted to the dance floor. This record was always a good catalyst. On this night the DJ was able to comply and so it was that on that mid-seventies night, in my brown checked suit and great barge like shoes with big heels, not really Glam Rock but certainly almost in fashion, I stomped away, Sandra, my wife, by my side. I was almost oblivious to anyone else. In fact it was only Sandra and me dancing.

Then, without prompting the DJ, he put on *Star, Star* a much underrated and underplayed record. If it had not been for the language (its original title is *Star Fucker)*, then it surely must have been a huge hit. This one of the stand out tracks on *Black & Blue* was a huge favourite of mine. Its Chuck Berry style guitar licks with strident chorus is really uplifting. I found myself dancing away and singing the words - not quite at the top of my voice but certainly very energetically. I suddenly realised that I was the only person on the dance floor and there was a gathering crowd of my colleagues watching and laughing. I haven't danced, in public, much since.

The second memorable part of the evening came towards the end. The Head Master, a cousin of the then current Archbishop of Canterbury, Donald Coggan, was about to leave with his wife. Rob, the pottery teacher, lurched up to her and took off the fur coat she had just put on, threw it over a chair and dragged her on to the dance floor. He proceeded to start dancing all around her, even though she must have been at least thirty years older than him. Bemused hardly sums up the expression on her face. The Head boldly rescued her, dragging her off even more roughly than Rob had done. Luckily it was the end of term and we all had the Christmas break to forget the events of the night. The Head Master retired shortly after, I suspect, still partly traumatised by the last official full staff Christmas Party we had for a number of years. The music of The Rolling Stones, I am sure, had not acted as a catalyst but you never know.

Balloon Debates

We used to have Balloon debates at lunchtime in Small Hall at Stanground College in the very early 80s. Each "contestant" played the role of a famous person arguing their worth to be kept in the balloon and not jettisoned as it plummeted downwards. Four or five each day voted for by audience (mainly year 11 and 6th form) Bernie (Head) appeared as God against me, as Mick Jagger, in the final two. Florence Nightingale, I recall, was one of the early victims. God played the omnipotent card and as creator of everything stated that he had the perfect right to stay in... or so he thought. I played the generation gap card, championing the cause of the youth of today through "my" music. I chomped my way through three Mars Bars. I don't even like them that much but had had no time for a school dinner - and won by a clear margin. God was not happy. This was a valid win for the counter culture ethic. This was in early 80s and the Stones were still regarded as outside the establishment by many. For those of you who believe that the Mars Bars addition was over the top, I do have to agree. I had never believed the salacious gossip from that time and there is overwhelming evidence now that the establishment was ganging up on The Rolling Stones at that time and that the story was actually made up by "The News Of The World". (See the upcoming section on the Redlands Drugs Bust for greater revelatory detail - page 78).

I made no reference at all to the chocolate bars while I made my plea to be kept in the balloon, relying purely on anyone who thought they knew the story to draw their own conclusions. It was merely a prop. A few of the staff, who were standing at the back, obviously knew the story – you could see it in their faces. One of my 6th form History students obviously also knew the story, and, without making any salacious comments himself, let me know that he understood the crude and, some might say, tasteless symbolism.

My main thrust was based on individualism and the future being led by the current generation of school children as they looked for a better world. I, or rather Jagger, was on their side championing their rights. It was a very decisive victory

I have to say that I am now ashamed of myself for resorting to such a lowdown Mars bar stunt but I did want to win... and I did. I liked to think that my argument was in tune with the student thinking.

The final two in the balloon

A Level History Student

On another school note, during an A Level History lesson on the Viet Nam war (since writing my History thesis on Ho Chi Minh and obtaining primary source material, I have always spelled Viet Nam as two words. It is not a typo) we were discussing the protest movement and the use of music from Dylan, Country Joe and the Fish ('give me an 'F' etc') of Woodstock fame and so on. Of course

The Rolling Stones were mentioned with "Paint It Black" and "Street Fighting Man" and the Grosvenor Square demo. Our Head Teacher, of Balloon debate infamy, had rather curiously mentioned, during a full school assembly, how he had been at this demo in 1968 as a student and kicked a police horse. We never found out if it kicked back… One of the students in the lesson -it was an all morning three-hour session interrupted only by break time - had come in a little late. Mark, had red hair which he had dyed that morning, or the night before, a bright green colour and he had on his CRASS T–Shirt and bondage trousers (no school uniform for 6th form at our place!). He made some comment in which he tried to intimate that he would have been a good and worthy protestor. One of the greatest put downs I have ever witnessed followed when Becky, the girl sitting to his left, looked at him, smiled, and said in a very matter of fact voice "And here you are studying for your A Levels. You little rebel, you". Mark would never have made a street fighting man.

1968 was a year littered with political protests in many countries in the world. It was probably the most tumultuous year of the century with assassinations (Martin Luther King, Jnr. and Robert Kennedy), and the overriding spirit of rebellion against the war in Viet Nam and the eastern bloc looking to shake off the mantle of communism (the short-lived Prague Spring in Czechoslovakia).

I had been a student in 1968 in my final year of teacher training and at Keele University, which oversaw my college at Madeley, there was a great deal of militancy during that year. I recall communist red flags being flown from several student buildings.

The USA had its problems with racism and civil rights, riots and overzealous policing and the increasing unpopular Viet Nam war at that time. There were protests, initially, at the campus of Columbus University, where hundreds of students occupied the buildings for several days. University officials then called in officers from the New York City Police, who broke up the demonstrations, beating and arresting hundreds of protestors. This took place at a time when nothing was sacrosanct to a world-wide TV audience. The student chant of "The whole world is watching" was there for everybody to witness.

This led to a wave of student activism throughout the world in 1968, including mass anti-war demonstrations in London, Poland, West Germany, Mexico, Italy and particularly in Paris, France. On 6 May, known as "Bloody Monday", students and police clashed in the Latin Quarter, Paris, resulting in hundreds of injuries. As the protests continued, millions of French workers went on strike in sympathy with the students.

The Rolling Stones recorded their single *Street Fighting Man* in May of that year and it doesn't take much to see where the inspiration from this came from. The specific event that prompted Mick Jagger to write the lyric was the demonstration at Grosvenor Square (close to the US Embassy) on 17 March, 1968. Jagger (along with Vanessa Redgrave – a known activist as well as a movie star) joined the estimated 25,000 protestors in condemning the Viet Nam War. Whether he bumped into my future head teacher will never be known.

The demonstrators marched to the embassy, where the protest became violent. Mounted police charged the crowd which responded by throwing rocks and smoke bombs.

This was the first real song that The Stones had recorded of an overt political nature. Jagger begins by singing "The time is right for fighting in the street" but has to admit with an air of hopelessness "but what can a poor boy do, 'cept sing in a rock and roll band". Bruce Springsteen told the writer Dave Marsh that "it is one of the greatest rock and roll lines of all time. It has that edge-of-the-cliff thing when you hit it. And it's funny; it's got humour to it." I, with many others, saw the song of exactly of its time and empathised with the thousands of students worldwide. Springsteen's view that it is the greatest lyric of all time is documented in Joe Taysom'sarticle in Far Out (January 2022). It is difficult to argue with The Boss!

It does need be stated that despite the Grosvenor Square demo, the public in the UK did not take the matter quite as seriously as in the USA and France. Jagger's "what can a poor boy do?" line showed that even he was not aiming to be a working-class hero.

Tariq Ali, a known left wing political extremist, had urged Jagger to write the song. It had originally been called *"Did Everyone Pay Their* Dues" (you can find it on YouTube). It seemed to be about abuse but with rather strange meanings; Jagger singing about an Indian chief and his family. Keith admitted that they were not too happy with the lyrics. The changed words, borne from the student unrest, sit much more comfortably especially with the strident nature of the music where the notes seem to tumble into each other. It is a song that projects menace that some critics have dubbed it as cosmetic rage but it was regarded by many at the time as a protest song.

In the USA, it was released as a single (from the *Beggars Banquet* album) on 31 August, just a few days after the Democratic National Convention in Chicago. The convention was marred by violence as the police clashed with protestors. Chicago's Mayor, Daley gave police the authority to "Shoot to kill any arsonist or anyone with a Molotov cocktail in his hand". Eleven people died during this hostile action and several hundred were injured. These scenes were broadcast live on Television. For the first time in any war the figures of soldiers killed and wounded were displayed every night on US TV screens in peoples' homes.

When the song was released, every radio station in Chicago (and most in the rest of the country) refused to play it for fear of inciting even more violence. There was no official ban as such but the stations knew that it was in their best interests to shun the song.. It, unsurprisingly, only reached number 48 in the US charts. Jagger, later, is reported to have said during an interview with Der Spiegel, the German magazine on its Culture page: "The radio stations that banned the song told me that *Street Fighting Man* was subversive. Of course it's subversive, we said, it's stupid to think that you can start a revolution with a record. I wish you could!"

In September 1970, during this interview, Jagger was also asked what he sang at his concerts with audiences in the many thousands: "Sie singen von Politik, Protest und

Revolution". (You sing of politics, protest and revolution). His response was "Ich singe nicht von Revolution" (I do not sing of revolution). He realised that you could not really change the world with a song even if you wanted to.

Despite only reaching number 21 in the UK, it did make the higher eschelons of the top ten in a number of western European countries. It is a song that has gained in status over the years and certainly helps to place the events of 1968 into context.

On a semi scholarly note I have run a number of music quizzes here in Greece to an expat audience, who, in the main are, like me, sixties teenagers. The quizzes mainly focus on music from the 1960s through the 1980s and sometimes beyond. There are always Rolling Stones questions though, out of fairness, I do include Beatles stuff too.

The following is an anagram of famous Stones' songs that I have used.

ROLLING STONES SONG ANAGRAMS

Solve these TEN Rolling Stones' Classic Song Anagrams. The number in brackets of each clue refers to the number of words in the answer.

TIP: Make a list of known Rolling Stones' songs FIRST & see if the letters match up to a song title below.

1 PET RATS UM (3) 1981
2 IN A FAST OCTIS (1) 1965
3 FISH MUCK GANJA LPJ (3) 1968
4 TIT BACK IN LAP (3) 1966
5 YON THOWN KNOKEM (3) 1969
6 FOFOT CLYDE OF GUM (5) 1965
7 WISH DROLES (2) 1971
8 WROB GANSUR (2) 1971
9 TROT IDOLER LESTER (3) 1965
10 RESIT VOWAL NOL (4) 1964
(Answers on page 179)

The Redlands Drugs Bust episode (February 1967)

The Rolling Stones, almost from the outset, were regarded as classic examples of the "sex, drugs and rock 'n' roll" mantra with especial reference to the drug issue. With Brian and Keith, in particular, there is little to deny. The now infamous Redlands episode shows how the establishment forces were keen to exert their will.

Having been a fan of The Rolling Stones from the outset, I was absolutely mortified when the news of the drug bust at Keith's Redlands home was made public. The whole situation seemed to be a "put up" job. I only discovered much later the reasoning behind the raid but was sufficiently suspicious at the time to know that this was grossly unfair. The trial and subsequent jailing of Jagger, Richards and Robert Fraser (an art dealer friend) was a travesty of the justice system. The sentences were far from commensurate with those that would have been handed to any non-celebrity. Photographs in the press of Jagger in handcuffs when he was being charged with the possession of just four amphetamine tablets were way over the top. Hindsight tells us that they were not even Jagger's but Marianne Faithfull's though he took the blame for the possession as they were found in his jacket pocket.

The whole situation served only to strengthen my feelings towards the group. I had still not seen the group live at this time but this made me want to whenever the chance arose. The tabloids had a field day with images of the handcuffed Jagger and Richards and tones of moral indignation. The broadsheets, too, were reporting the incident in detail though not in such a lurid way.

George Harrison (a Beatle, and therefore "a nice guy," with his wife Patti), and a friend of Keiths had, I believe, been at the Redlands party just before the heavy-handed police raid and he always claimed that the police had waited until he left the premises before they made their move. The Establishment at work.

One area where there was strong support for Jagger and Richards was the pirate radio ships. I used to listen to Radio Caroline which used to dedicate large slots for Rolling Stones' music. Radio London, too, with its Kenny and Cash Show (Kenny Everett and Dave Cash) was a favourite. Everett, a Liverpudlian, naturally favoured the Beatles but Dave Cash used to redress the balance with Rolling Stones offerings. This support from the pirates was welcome. I discovered from reading Simon Well's excellent book –*The Great Rolling* Stones *Drug Bust* – that while Keith was incarcerated in his cell, he heard a Stones song *It's All Over Now* via the radios in the cells. It appeared that everyone with coincidental irony had tuned into the same station and had turned the volume up.

Wells' book also details what a great many suspected at the time – the involvement of *The News Of The World* newspaper. Poor reporting had mistaken Brian Jones in a drug related incident for Jagger and it had printed a story about Mick which was obviously totally wrong. When the NOTW discovered that Jagger was going to sue the newspaper – and they realised that they were in the wrong and would lose – they seized upon an opportunity to discredit Jagger in a revengeful bid to halt his claim. Somebody tipped the newspaper off about the weekend party at Redlands and the NOTW was instrumental in informing the police who carried out the raid.

This is not the place to go into all the details of the raid but the salacious story about Jagger, Marianne Faithfull and the Mars Bar do need to be explained. It was claimed that Jagger was feasting on the infamous Mars Bar that was placed in Marianne's vagina. Wells has scrupulously scrutinised all of the police note books and relevant paperwork from the raid and there is not one single reference to this act with the confectionary anywhere. He rightly deduces that this story was the fabrication of the NOTW. It would have been the talk of the station if it had really happened. It was not mentioned anywhere in the immediate aftermath of the raid. Faithfull's wearing of only a bearskin rug certainly also seems to have been exaggerated in order to titillate the story though she had just had a bath.

In the light of the phone hacking activities undertaken by this newspaper in much later times leading to its eventual and rightful enforced closure, the malicious involvement and reporting appear to have been quite standard practice.

One thing that did result from the ultimate freeing of the two Rolling Stones (after spending a small time behind bars) was a great tongue in cheek video that accompanied the song *We Love You* written in the aftermath of the case.

The single opens with the sounds of entry into jail, and a cell door clanging shut and pounding piano. The song's lyric, has been regarded as a spoof on the Beatles' *All You Need Is Love*. When one examines the lyrics closely a strong anti-establishment posture is evident:

"we don't care if you hound "we"
and lock the doors around "we"......
"you will never win "we",
your uniforms don't fit "we"
you're dead and then we're in."

Images of the Stones in the courtroom with Richards as the bewigged judge holding up a bearskin rug with Marianne looking on, adds to the preceding events. As a diehard fan I really empathised with this anti-establishment stance and wallowed in the victory.

Despite the tabloid condemnation of the morally decadent Rolling Stones there surprising support from one area. *The Times* newspaper with an editorial by William Rees-Mogg – "Who Breaks A Butterfly On A Wheel?" This editorial was highly critical of the court's verdict - three months in jail for Jagger and twelve for Richards and is regarded as being instrumental in the successful appeal by the nonplussed Stones. Marianne Faithfull reported that Jagger was in tears and very distraught after receiving the verdict and quite a justifiable reaction under the circumstances in my mind.

Rees-Mogg's triumphant editorial concludes thus: "If we are going to make any case a symbol of the conflict between the sound traditional values of Britain and the

WHO BREAKS A BUTTERFLY ON A WHEEL?

new hedonism, then we must be sure that the sound traditional values include those of tolerance and equity. It should be the particular quality of British justice to ensure that Mr. Jagger is treated exactly the same as anyone else, no better and no worse. There must remain a suspicion in this case that Mr. Jagger received a more severe sentence than would have been thought proper for any purely anonymous young man."

Fancy words but very appropriate but this was not the end to the story. One of my college courses was Film and we were studying documentaries and news programmes as a module with specific reference to *World in Action* and *Panorama*. We were encouraged to make notes on anything that we saw during a typical week for use in an assignment later.

After the jail sentence was quashed ITV's *World in Action* featured Jagger and an incongruous group of establishment figures including William Rees-Mogg himself. On the lawn of a stately home, Jagger was helicoptered in very dramatically – almost SAS style. My notes at that time refer to a rather limp programme in which the helicopter was probably the most interesting bit. The programme was actually screened during the Summer break and, to be honest, I almost certainly would not have watched, nor made notes, had it not featured Mick Jagger. He gave a short, press style statement and then joined in conversations with the Rev Thomas Corbishley - a Jesuit priest, Dr. John Robinson – The Bishop of Woolwich and Lord Stow Hill who was a former Labour Home Secretary.

The conversation was quite stilted, and Jagger came across as a rather earnest, young man. I am sure that Andrew Loog Oldham would have been very upset at this image that was being projected by his supposedly subversive rebel. I did note, perhaps too facetiously, that all that was missing was a plate of cucumber sandwiches.

However, I never did use my scriblings in the ensuing assignment.

Toronto 1977

I suppose the most serious drug offence took place in Toronto, Canada in 1977 when Keith was arrested while asleep. He was charged with possession and trafficking. "They couldn't wake me. By law you have to be conscious to be arrested,'' Richards dryly recollects in his 2010 autobiography *Life*. "My memory of it is waking up and them going slap, slap, two Mounties dragging me about the room, slapping me. Trying to get me conscious...''

This was a serious matter and, with a minimum seven year sentence a real prospect, could have destroyed the group. I recall waiting for news as to what was going to happen because this did seem genuinely serious. To cut what was a long story short, Richards was eventually given a suspended sentence and ordered to give a benefit concert. He had embarked on a drug rehabilitation course and this was taken into account at the court case several months later. There was speculation in the press that this could end the group and I remember feeling very relieved when the sentence was finally reached.

Adding to the notoriety of the group while they were in Canada, Margaret Trudeau, who was a big fan of the group, attended parties hosted by The Stones and was spotted wearing just a bathrobe, at The Stones hotel, giving credence to the fact that she was "seeing" Mick Jagger although recent research indicates that it was, in fact, she and Ronnie Wood who were very close.

If the group had been forced to fold then we would never have been treated to "*Some Girls* from the following year -1978. Those critics who had written The Stones off, would have had to eat their words as this album was not only a commercial success it was critically acclaimed. I believe it was the first Stones album to be nominated for a Grammy and it is one of the highest selling records from the group with sales of well over 11 million to date world wide. (*Blue and Lonesome* did finally win a Grammy for Best Traditional Blues Album in 2016).

We would also not have had the pleasure of their many magnificent concert tours since that time either.

My Son Christian and Ronnie Wood

My son manufactured the Balloon debate picture of Jagger and God and has always had an artistic bent. The day in August 1976 when we took him home from Peterborough Maternity Unit to our house in Yaxley, Cambridgeshire, I was very keen to have him noise trained. As an eleven-and-a-half-pound baby he was already very alert. I put my stereo headphones on him and wanted to play a Stones song for him but the first album I came across was *Abraxas* by Santana. He listened intently to *Samba Pa Ti* - a gentle, rhythmic number. I did play *Memory Motel* from *Black and Blue* the following day. Of course he later had all the nursery rhymes but I wanted to ground him properly.

Chris got to love his music. He has written some excellent songs and is a very accomplished guitar player. We used to watch Top of The Pops together and he would join in some of the songs that he knew. The Pretenders song *Brass in Pocket* was a particular favourite where he used to sing out the *special, so special* part along with Chrissie Hynde.

While watching another music programme on TV in 1983, the group Twisted Sister appeared, playing their cover version of The Stones song *It's Only Rock 'n' Roll (But I Like It)*. Chris, aged about six, was really fascinated by the song and probably more by the lead singer, a Bette Midler, pantomime dame lookalike, Dee Snider. His long, blonde, curly locks were well in keeping with the Glam Rock scene. Chris, who liked to draw character types, found his best green felt tipped pen and drew a picture of what he had seen. We played this game where I sang *I know, it's only rock 'n' roll* and he responded *But I Like it*. We did this many times - sometimes even swapping roles. I have to say that at age 36 as I was at the time, a supposedly responsible adult, it was probably more in keeping with my son's age but I have to say...I like it!

Then, quite naturally and unsurprisingly, I located my LP with the title of the song and played track three from Side One several times so that he could hear the definitive and, naturally, best version of the song. I kept the drawing along with many other examples of his artistic prowess in an ever growing folder that monitors the progress of his life. The picture is reproduced below:

There is one more really hands on involvement with Chris and The Rolling Stones that I will be eternally grateful for. Enter Mister Ronnie Wood.

Ronnie Wood's autograph

Chris, who works in programme development in TV and has written a number of very successful shows, has met very many A, B and C list celebrities. He encountered Ronnie Wood in a coffee bar in Primrose Hill. He is unfazed by seeing and talking to famous people.

Ronnie had split from his wife and was currently seeing a Russian model.

Chris went across to Ronnie, who was with Ekaterina, and announced: "I don't usually do this sort of thing but my dad is an absolutely gigantic Rolling Stones fan. Would you mind signing an autograph for him?" Without hesitation, Ronnie signed a piece of paper as can be seen in the copy reproduced. He asked my name and duly penned a really clear autograph – unlike the undecipherable scribbles that the tennis players seem to do at the end of a match.

Chris engaged him in conversation about the paparazzi that were waiting outside the coffee bar saying that he sympathized about the amount of attention he was getting. Ronnie was very level headed in his response acknowledging that there was little you could do except grin and bear it. It doesn't pay you to antagonise them.

Chris went back to his friends continued drinking his coffee. He was alerted by a pat on the shoulder several minutes later. Ronnie, who was leaving, came over to him and said, "Give my best regards to Mike", smiled, and walked out.

It is this second act that didn't need to be done that endears me to Ronnie who was in the thick of a popular press "mini-soap opera" with his relationships at the time and didn't have to go that extra step. Naturally, Chris rang me to say: "Guess who I met today?" When he then contacted me the next day and asked if I had seen the newspapers, I had to say "no". We were staying with my mother-in-law and she had a copy of the Daily Mail. Inside was the article and picture of Ronnie and Ekaterina taken at Primrose Hill the same morning that I had "obtained" the autograph.

I was pleased when, years later, Ronnie stopped his drinking. His playing has really matured. He also settled down after his marriage to Jo broke up and has a beautiful set of twin girls with his new wife Sally. He has cetainly mellowed and his artwork continues to flourish.

The story in the press the next day. The Daily Mail April 22, 2009

Earl's Court Concert May 1976. A major indoor event as part of the successful European Tour that year and the first time I had been able to properly see The Stones.

The Rolling Stones played six concerts at Earls Court Arena at the end of May, 1976. I went to the second night on Saturday 22nd May. The *Black & Blue* album had recently been released and the set list reflected this. *Black & Blue* was a really funky record. The producer was the wonderfully named Arif Mardin. The fact that the brilliantly exuberant Billy Preston was an ever-present member of the entourage at the concerts attested to that. *Hey Negrita*, a reggae tinged, up-tempo number really rocked as did *Star Star*. It was during this song that a giant inflatable phallus arose from the stage to be ridden by Mick Jagger. It was apparently nicknamed "The Tired Grandfather," due to its general inability to stay erect. I don't recall it deflating during the performance I saw however. The puritan element of the establishment would not have approved I am sure. Jagger also threw several buckets of water into the crowd during the concert. This was the start of bigger and bigger special effects at their concerts more of which later. The stage, small by later concerts' standards, was, nonetheless a major talking point

The show had opened with a huge hydraulically operated Lotus style flower that Jagger appeared from as Keith's guitar sounded the unmistakable riff for *Honky Tonk Women*. The petals reached out to the crowd. It was like a six-pointed star. I had certainly never seen anything like it before. The excitement, as this familiar and well-loved classic song started up, was almost ear shattering.

Billy Preston contributed two numbers with the *Outta Space* instrumental being a standout. Preston played the organ and also danced quite frenetically – all arms and legs – Jagger joined in and the two danced together around the stage, Preston and certainly made a lasting impression. I can even forgive him that he also played with The Beatles.

On the downside, the acoustics at the Earl's Court Arena were not that brilliant. The sound was undoubtedly loud. I have seen concert footage of the event and The Stones were good. Some of the sound, however, was not. This was not down to them but the venue. I discovered some time later that the reason the Stones appeared at the Knebworth Festival that August was to atone for what had been a disappointment to them and their fans for the poor sound quality. Alas, I was not there.

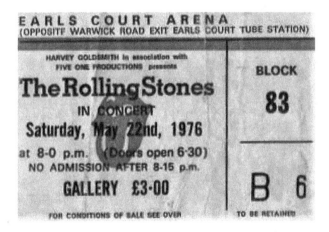

Look at the price of this ticket a very modest £3.00. Yes, there were more expensive tickets but when one examines the price range of tickets and the hospitality packages that exist in 2019 on the No Filter Tour this price seems almost like a giveaway. It was, however, £3.00 more than I had paid for the 1969 Hyde Park gig!

STNES MISCELLANY #3

Earl's Court Set List:

Honky Tonk Women
If You Can't Rock Me / Get Off of My Cloud
Hand of Fate
Hey Negrita
Ain't Too Proud to Beg
Fool to Cry
Hot Stuff
Star Star
You Gotta Move
You Can't Always Get What You Want
Happy
Tumbling Dice
Nothing from Nothing
Outta Space
Midnight Rambler
It's Only Rock 'n' Roll (But I Like It)
Brown Sugar
Jumpin' Jack Flash
Street Fighting Man
Sympathy for the Devil

1982 Saturday 26 June Wembley Stadium

This was the third time that I had seen The Stones and the nearest to the front of the stage that I ever managed.

I journeyed to London with my mate, Alex, from Huntingdon Railway Station. My first memory of the day is of an elderly gentleman, with a deer stalker hat precariously perched on his head, who took exception to me moving very quickly across the platform to get onto the train in a bid to get a seat. "You bounder! You cad!" he shouted at me waving his walking stick as I rushed past him. This encounter with a character from Jeeves and Wooster has been the source of many a laugh in the days since. Once we were aboard the train we discovered that there were no seats in the regular compartment. We walked into the next and found the same. As we were destined to be on our feet for most of the day, we found our way into the First-Class carriage. We slid the door to our empty compartment shut behind us and sat opposite one another in a vain bid to make it look full. A short while later the ticket collector arrived. He was a short man with red curly hair. He asked for our tickets in a most obsequious manner. After briefly perusing our paper-work, he looked up and announced: "You do realise that this is a First-Class compartment, don't you?" In unison, Alex (a six-foot four ex second row rugby forward) and I stood up. I am a mere six foot, but a quite burly, ex prop forward. We looked down at the inspector and replied in unison: "Yes, we do!" His response was a curt "Right then. Just letting you know" and he left, sliding the door shut behind him. My second fit of laughter for the day. Our second fit of laughter for the day. It was going to be a good one.

We had bought with us an array of filled rolls and pork pies as well as a good amount of Ruddles County beer cans to help sustain through what was going to be a long day. We managed to down a few cans before the train pulled into King's Cross Station and a pie (or two) of course.

We made good progress via the underground and ar-rived at Wembley by mid-morning. We still had four cans of Ruddles left as we approached the gateway that was indicated on our tickets. "Very sorry but you cannot take any drink into the stadium" was the first thing we were greeted with when our pack up bags were inspected. Was this guy the brother of the train inspector and he was seeking revenge? No, it was policy for everyone we were informed. Alex and I looked at one another and without speaking we both flipped the ring pull on a can and downed the beer. By the time that we had finished the second can each we were feeling a little full. We would go to the loo inside and so we entered the stadium after having our tickets checked.

The first thing we saw inside was a huge array of bars and drink being served. It wasn't beer per se that that was being forbidden outside – it was our beer. More profit for the stadium and the organisers. Loads of people were drinking weak beer from flimsy plastic glasses.

It was still mid-morning and the concert was not due to start for at least a couple of hours. After paying a visit to the loo, we looked towards the stage and saw that there were very few people standing in front. We made our way as far as we could and were only about ten metres from the front right in the centre.. If we could keep these places then we were going to have a great view of everything. Leaving to go to the loo again would pose a problem. Once the concert got underway and the crowds began to fill up behind us, almost as far as we could see, we knew that we were going to stay there. Some people had devised a cunning way of relieving themselves without having to move. A number of plastic carrier bags tied tightly and full of piss were thrown into the air in a huge looping motion. As they landed and usually burst open this was greeted with a huge cheer from all those assembled near but not touched by the exploding contents. I remember thinking several times "Please God, not me" as every launch took place. Alex and I remained rather fortuitously, but gratefully unscathed, nonetheless.

It was a very hot day and we drank in moderation. Once The Stones came on, we were aware of a strange smell. We turned in unison to see this smelly, young git who had a very thin light brown suede headband despite having quite short hair. The stench of body odour was the cause of the smell. He kept shouting "Mick! Mick!" and pleading for a particular song which was never answered successfully. He then asked us to move because his sister was right at the front and he attempted to push past. Again, in unison, we both stuck out elbows which blocked his attempt. I told him that my sister was at the front, too, along with my mother but we were not going to move. We were happy where we were. He realised that he was not going to get any nearer and backed off and we never saw nor smelled him again.

Bill had a bandana tied around his head and a neckerchief on which we could clearly see the pattern. His bass guitar lines were great especially during *Miss You*. Really thumping. Rib rocking. He had a really long cigarette almost stuck to his lips. Ronnie, too, I seem to recall was smoking. Keith seemed immersed in his traditional riff making mode – concentrating yet having fun.The group's clothing, especially Jagger's, was very kindergarten - romper room in style. Many bright colours - Mick sported red and white thick striped tights (well they weren't what you could call trousers). This was the eighties and an era that is noted for its extravagant, dare I say, outrageous, fashion.

The support acts were The J. Geils band and Black Uhuru. (See the flyer reproduced below). Both support bands performed very good sets. J. Geils did "Centrefold" which had been a top three record earlier in the year. They were the more widely known of the support acts, but it was Black Uhuru, who, I had to confess I had not heard of, who proved to be a particularly great and lasting delight.

Even to this day I play their "Liberation" double CD compilation with wonderful stand-out tracks like *What is Life, Youth of Eglington* and *Chill Out.*

Without their inclusion by The Stones, I may never had taken notice of this fine reggae ensemble who easily rivalled Bob Marley And The Wailers at that time. Michael Rose, their Jamaican lead singer, who had constantly mixed with Sly and Robbie, Gregory Isaacs, Dennis Brown and the aforementioned Wailers on the island, possessed a truly great and wide ranging voice. He was part of the reggae elite.

There was another Rolling Stones link in that Keith Richards had played guitar on an earlier Michael Rose solo recording of *Guess Who's Coming To Dinner* and *Shine Eye Gal.*

Information Sheet

THIS IS WEMBLEY AND TODAY YOU WILL SEE THE GREATEST ROCK 'N' ROLL BAND IN THE WORLD!

Lee Cooper

PRESENTS

THE ROLLING STONES

BLACK UHURU ARE OPENING THE SHOW AND SHOULD GET YOU DANCING, AND THEN THE J. GEILS BAND WILL KEEP YOU ON YOUR FEET AND ROCKIN'. AND YOU CAN TRY YOUR HAND AT THE TEASER AND QUIZES IN THE INTERVALS!

NOW THAT YOU ARE HERE, TAKE A MOMENT TO READ THIS LEE COOPER INFORMATION LEAFLET, AND THEN – ENJOY YOURSELVES!

There are full Red Cross facilities, Police, Fire Brigade and Security for your safety. Wheelchairs may go into the Stadium with an ordinary ticket through the gate at the Players Tunnel, where they will be shown through to the arena. Toilets for disabled persons are located in the toilet compound by the Royal Tunnel, inside the Stadium.

Bottles, cans, cameras and recording equipment are not allowed inside the Stadium.

Hot and cold food and soft drink bars are open inside the Stadium all day, and licensed bars are open during normal licensing hours. Drinking water taps are sited around the Stadium.

The Concert finishes at 10pm on Friday 25th and 9pm on Saturday 26th June, and extra Trains, Buses and Tubes have been arranged to help you get home.

TRAINS – From Wembley Central Station to either Euston or Watford and from Wembley Complex to Marylebone.

TUBES – From Wembley Park Station on the Jubilee Line to London or Stanmore and on the Metropolitan Line to London or Uxbridge.

BUSES – From the Stadium No's 83-92-182. From the Triangle No. 18. From Wembley Park Station No. 297.

Any lost property will be placed with Wembley Stadium Security. Write to: Wembley Stadium, Wembley, Middlesex HA9 0DW with any enquiries.

BRITISH RAIL TELEPHONES FOR SERVICES

EUSTON/BROAD STREET/(MARYLEBONE/ST PANCRAS)   01-387 7070
MOORGATE/KING'S CROSS   01-278 2477
PADDINGTON   01-262 6767
FENCHURCH STREET/LIVERPOOL STREET   01-283 7171
BLACKFRIARS/CANNON STREET/CHARING CROSS
HOLBORN VIADUCT/LONDON BRIDGE/VICTORIA
WATERLOO   01-928 5100

TAXI SERVICES

BAKER STREET STATION   935-3553
BRIXTON OVAL   774-3552
HARROW/HEATH   148-1016
SLOANE SQUARE   730-2964
RADIO TAXICABS (SOUTHERN)   272-0256
CAMBRIDGE CIRCUS CAR HIRE   734-9603
ALDBN CAR SERVICE   928-6181
WEMBLEY RADIO CARS   903-3326
WEMBLEY & HEADSER LANE   455-2595
O.A.S. CARS   903-7137
YELLOW CARS   903-5353

PETROL (24 HOUR SERVICE)

CHELSEA CLOISTERS – Sloane Avenue SW3 – 589-0220
CRISMOR FLYOVER SERVICE STATION – 1 West Road W4 – 994-1119
SAVENDISH MOTORS/Cavendish Road NW6 – 655-0040
ESSO GARAGES – 170/177 James Vale W6 – 386-7321
ESSO GARAGE – 617 Finchley Road NW3 – 435-2354
FOUNTAIN – Mawson Lane W4 – 994-2446
MOONS MOTORS – 23/31 Saunton Place NW1 – 720-7221
PARK LANE UNDERGROUND GARAGE CAR PARK – 262-1814
STATION SUPREME – Fortune Green Road NW7 – 435-2251

WEMBLEY POLICE STATION – 01-900 7212

 Please remember the local residents, and take care not to disturb or litter the neighbourhood; let's keep Wembley Complex in everyone's good books for entertainment events in times to come.

DAIHATSU

Inside the Stadium, the Daihatsu Information Point is at the opposite end to the stage, on the Flame Platform, for any answers you need, or friends you want to meet up with or leave messages for –

ONCE INSIDE, EVERY TICKET GIVES FREE ACCESS THROUGHOUT THE STADIUM

1. DAIHATSU INFORMATION POINT
2. RED CROSS CENTRE
3. ROYAL TUNNEL TOILETS WITH FACILITIES FOR THE DISABLED
4. FEMALE TOILETS IN N COMPOUND

— BRIDGES FOR ARENA
= ENTRY AND EXIT

The following facilities will be available within Wembley Stadium all day –
Drinking water
Hot and cold catering
Red Cross mobile and auxiliary posts

Do you know?

1. WHICH TOWNS AND WHAT VENUES DID THE STONES PLAY IN THE UK LAST MONTH BEFORE THE START OF THIS EUROPEAN TOUR?
2. WHEN WAS THE STONES FIRST AMERICAN TOUR AND WHO SHARED THE BILL WITH THEM?
3. WHAT WAS THE STONES FIRST SELF PENNED HIT?
4. WHAT WAS THE STONES FIRST ORIGINAL ALBUM?
5. WHAT IS THE NAME OF THE SHOW THE STONES MADE THEIR TV DEBUT ON?
6. WHERE DID MICK JAGGER AND KEITH RICHARD FIRST MEET?
7. WHAT MARVIN GAYE SONG DID THE STONES RECORD?
8. IN WHICH AUSTRALIAN FILM DID MICK JAGGER APPEAR IN 1979?
9. WHICH STONES ALBUM HAD A 3-D COVER?
10. WHAT COLLEGE WAS MICK JAGGER ATTENDING AT THE TIME HE BECAME A MUSICIAN?
11. WHAT BAND DID MICK JAGGER SING WITH BEFORE THE STONES?
12. ON WHICH "LET IT BLEED" TRACK DOES KEITH RICHARD SING HIS FIRST LEAD VOCAL?
13. WHO PLAYED PIANO, FRENCH HORN AND ORGAN ON "YOU CAN'T ALWAYS GET WHAT YOU WANT"?
14. WHICH BAND DID RONNIE WOOD PLAY WITH BEFORE HE JOINED THE STONES?
15. WHAT YEAR DID RONNIE BEGIN TOURING WITH THE STONES?
16. WHAT WAS THE ROLLING STONES FIRST NUMBER ONE SINGLE ON ROLLING STONES RECORDS?
17. WHAT RELEASED AS A DISCO SINGLE WAS A WORLDWIDE HIT IN 1978?
18. THE SINGLE "YOU GOT TO WALK AND DON'T LOOK BACK" WAS RECORDED IN 1979 WITH WHOM?
19. WHAT STONES SONG OPENED AND CLOSED THE FILM "COMING HOME"?
20. THE IDEA FOR THE SONG "SYMPATHY FOR THE DEVIL" CAME FROM WHAT BOOK?
21. NAME THE OTHER TWO BRITISH STADIUMS THE STONES ARE PLAYING IN THIS TOUR?
22. NAME THE THREE MUSICIANS PLAYING WITH THE STONES ON THIS TOUR?
23. NAME AT LEAST 23 OF THE ORIGINAL "ENGLISH INVASION" GROUPS WHO WENT TO AMERICA BEFORE 1966?
24. HOW MANY WORDS CAN YOU CREATE FROM THE LETTERS IN "ROLLING STONES"?

Compiled by JOE SCANNELLA

ON THE STREETS LEE COOPER MEAN JEANS

Were you right?

JUMPIN' JACK FLASH and THE MIDNIGHT RAMBLER
THERE ARE 37 TITLES OF STONES SONGS IN THIS STORY. CAN YOU FIND THEM ALL, AND, IF SO, CAN YOU SING THEM ALL?

"So me and my partner, Jumpin' Jack Flash, we was walkin' along one dark, starry winter night, an' he said to me, "Midnight Rambler, m'man, it's a sad day an' I don't know why, but right now I just don't know what to do." I said to him, "Listen Jack, stop breakin' down, don't let's just sit here confessin' the blues, let's go out an' get us some girls stayin' here is yesterday's papers, man, so let's head down the road apiece 'an Flash, he's sayin', "I dunno, man, I got the blues, honest I do, feel like ol' tome there singin' the stray cat blues." But I says, "I know what this street fightin' man needs", and I says, "Jack, you gotta move and get happy before you have your nineteenth nervous breakdown"! Now down at 2120 South Michigan Ave. is this little dive, and I know we're gonna find some honky tonk women. I said, "Come on, can't you hear the music? Everybody needs somebody to love". I see he's torn and frayed, so I head up to my ol' friend Sweet Virginia and say, "I need you baby, you got the silver that me Jack has to have". She looked at him and said "Listen here, little red rooster, I ain't a factory girl". But then she smiled sweetly. And Jack says "We're wastin' time, so do you want to dance, little sister?" and she says yeah, little by little they startin' to sway, and she softly says to Jack, "Shake your hips, dude, and set it loose!""

THE ROLLING STONES

(IN DID YOU GET ALL OF THESE?)

ROLL, RENT, ROLE, TOLL, TROLL, STROLL, RING, LION, OR, REST, NEST, TONE, GONE, GOON, LOOSE, GOOSE, NOOSE, SHORT, SINGER, STING, NOSE, STONE, LINE, SLING, LINGO, SONG, SISTER, LINT, TIN, TOIL, OIL, SLOT, TOP, LOG, LONG, SORE, TIT, NUT, NOT, SOON, LORE, TELLER, NINE, NIT, NOON, LOT, TELL, N.E, TALL, SLO, SLO, TINT, LOST, ISLE, LINGER, RENT,

AND LEST YOU SHOULD GIVE UP THERE ARE HUNDREDS MORE!

ABERDEEN CAPITOL THEATRE, GLASGOW APOLLO, EDINBURGH PLAYHOUSE AND THE 100 CLUB IN LONDON. 2 SEPTEMBER 1964. THE EVERLY BROTHERS AND THE WAS BO DIDDLEY. 3 THE LAST TIME. 4 AFTERMATH. 5 THANK YOUR LUCKY STARS. 6 MARPOLE COUNTY PRIMARY SCHOOL WHEN THEY WERE SIX YEARS OLD. 7 HITCH HIKE. 8 OUT OF OUR HEADS. 9 RED KILLER. 10 THE LONDON SCHOOL OF ECONOMICS. 11 ALEXIS KORNER'S BLUES INCORPORATED. 12 YOU GOT THE SILVER. 13 AL KOOPER. 14 THE FACES. 15 1975 —TOUR OF AMERICA. 16 BROWN SUGAR IN 1971. 17 MISS YOU. 18 PETER TOSH. 19 OUT OF TIME. 20 THE MASTER AND MARGARITA BY MIKHAIL BULAKOV. 21 NEWCASTLE UNITED F.C. ON WEDNESDAY 23rd JUNE, AND BRISTOL CITY F.C. ON SUNDAY 27th JUNE. 22 IAN STEWART, IAN McLAGAN AND BOBBY KEYES. 23 THE ANIMALS, DAVE CLARK FIVE, FREDDIE AND THE DREAMERS, GERRY AND THE PACEMAKERS, HERMAN'S HERMITS, THE HOLLIES, THE KINKS, MANFRED MANN, THE MOODY BLUES, THE SEARCHERS, PETER AND GORDON, THE PRETTY THINGS, THE BEATLES, THE SEEKERS, THE SMALL FACES, SPENCER DAVIS GROUP, THEN, THE TROGGS, THE WHO, THE YARDBIRDS, WAYNE FONTANA AND THE MINDBENDERS, THE ZOMBIES AND OF COURSE, THE ROLLING STONES. 24 TELL, TIE, TELL, SLO, SLOT, TINT, LOST...

Being so close to the front did not spoil the sound. I had had misgivings. Being that near to the stack of speakers had made me wonder and I remember saying to Alex that we might have appreciated the sound if we had been a little further back but the thrill of seeing them in close up outweighed any doubts we might have had. The Stones played a very strong set of songs and I particularly enjoyed (as I still do today) the *Beast of Burden* song. The show just built and built with the final array of songs being among everyone's favourites. The crowd's enjoyment spilled over into a cacophonous roar as the fireworks that ended the performance exploded in the darkening sky above the stage. This was by far the strongest performance that I had seen from the group. They were still the tops for me. We travelled home very tired but elated to have been witness to a great concert.

ST⦿NES MISCELLANY #4

Wembley Set List:
Under My Thumb
When the Whip Comes Down
Let's Spend The Night Together
Shattered
Neighbours
Black Limousine
Just My Imagination (Running Away With Me)
Twenty Flight Rock
Going to a Go-Go
Chantilly Lace
Let Me Go
Time Is on My Side
Beast of Burden

Let It Bleed
You Can't Always Get What You Want
Little T&A
Tumbling Dice Hang Fire
Miss You
Honky Tonk Women Brown Sugar
Start Me Up
Jumpin' Jack Flash
(I Can't Get No) Satisfaction

ST●NES MISCELLANY #5

Rolling Stones Firsts

Despite the ongoing jokes about their age, one reason that I have rally admired The Stones is that they have been at the forefront of technology with regard to music and performance. Some of their "firsts" may not be that salubrious but, overall, they have paved the way for others to follow. The following list exemplifies this.

First band to be caught urinating in public at a petrol station against a wall after being refused a toilet. The ensuing court case resulted in a 15 guinea fine for the three offending band members. The public were apparently scandalised by such behaviour. 1965

First blues record to reach Number One (and the only one, thus far) with *Little Red Rooster*. It was also the first record by a British band to be banned in the USA because of "objectionable lyrics". 1965

First music artist (Keith Richards) to be ordered to play two free concerts in lieu of the usual minimum seven year prison sentence after importing narcotics into

Canada. The band played Toronto after 22 grams of heroin were found in his hotel room. 1977

First British band to receive a Lifetime Achievement award at the Grammys 1986 (The Beatles were not given this award until 2014)

First to broadcast (streaming) 20 minutes of live audio and video from a performance in Dallas the week before. The Stones were the first major rock band to broadcast on the internet. 1994

Bill Gates and Mick Jagger struck a deal for the use of *Start Me Up* to launch Windows 95. Reported as anywhere between $8 million and $14 million, it was probably much nearer $4million – which is still a major deal for the Stones. 1995

Biggest ever deal of corporate sponsorship when Sprint (long distance carrier firm) paid £2.5 million to print its name on tickets and stage banners 1997

First rock band to play in Communist Russia. They had applied in 1967 to perform in Moscow but were banned when Soviet officials saw them play in Warsaw, Poland and did not approve. 1998

The Bigger Bang Tour set a record in grossing £115 million in receipts over 147 dates in less than four months. Overall the two year tour earned a massive £395 million and was the highest grossing tour of all time until eclipsed by U2's 360 Degree Tour in 2009-11. 2005-6

First international rock band to play a gig in China. They had been regarded as the potent symbols of decadent western capitalism during the Cultural Revolution

1966-67. When finally performing they had to cut five songs with suggestive lyrics from their set list. The show was screened by the Chinese state broadcaster CCTV – another first. 2006

First appearance at iconic Glastonbury considered the best ever show by a reigning British rock band and by organiser Michael Eavis as "the high spot of 43 years of Glastonbury" 2014

First British rock group to perform at a free concert in Havana, Cuba. Their music had always been deemed as an "ideological deviation" until Raoul Castro allowed the event to take place just three days after Barrack Obama, the US President, had visited the island. 2016

Although slightly less lucrative than the group's previous trek around the globe, the latest figures have made The Stones the only band to appear twice on Billboard's list of the top 10 grossing tours in history, as well as the first group to gross more than $400 million on two separate tours.

2005-07 Bigger Bang Tour $ 558,255,524 2017-19 No Filter Tour $416,000,000 2021 No Filter US Tour $115.500,000.

This latter tour consisted of just 14 concerts due to the Covid impact on events and it was the highest grossing by any music act in 2021.

There are other areas that The Stones have had firsts in for stage and set design, blimps, camera drones etc. They are truly innovative and summing up these all of these firsts, perhaps the most innovative band in history. The template that others have been happy to follow.

Wembley Stadium Concert 4 July 1990

This was the first time that I had seen the group for eight years. The 1980s had not been so kind to Mick and the boys. There was not, unsurprisingly, much anticipation. I did feel a touch of trepidation. Some in the press were happy to deride them. They were seen to be 'past' it.

Gun was the support act. They were a hard rock group from Glasgow, Scotland. I can only remember their song *Better Days* from their performance. Unless the support act is outstanding it is often likely that they will not easily be remembered. They were no Black Uhuru!

After a huge tour of the USA, Japan and Europe The Stones had headed for the UK. They were scheduled to do five nights at Wembley. I was going to the first of these nights with slight apprehension. Would they be burnt out after such a massive tour? They had been in semi- retirement for the years leading up to this tour. I need not have worried. They were in top form with Jagger as sassy as ever. The very wide walkways on either side of the stage seemed to stretch for miles and Jagger was almost sprinting from side to side during some numbers. They were even better than in 1982. The mass of dates had acted to sharpen their performances. I need not have worried. They were in absolute, top form. I have heard it said that Jagger ran about ten miles during each concert in his heyday.

It was the same night as the England v West Germany infamous penalty shoot-out match in the semi finals of the FIFA World Cup. I would always have plumped for The Stones concert rather than watch the football on TV. The game finished 1-1 after extra time but England lost on penalties. Jagger kept disappearing for moments between numbers and was apparently keeping tabs on the score. I seem to recall that he even gave the score out. Later, the German manager was told that Mick Jagger was now backing Germany to win the World Cup. He winced "You can't bet on (his) predictions because by backing England at the start he has been wrong about football before". Jagger's switched allegiance proved correct, however, with the German team defeating Argentina in the final.

It was on a school night albeit towards the end of the Summer term, so the journey by train to London was quite circumspect. It was then by tube to Wembley, where the hordes of fans milling about seemed huge. We had seats in one of the stands halfway back on the left hand side. We had a good view of the stage. No more standing near the front in the crowd now that I was in my forties. Of course most people still stood up when they were playing but you did have the option of a seat.

The band took the stage amid crackling fireworks and roaring flame towers - both of which would become *de rigueur* on future tours. A mighty cheer from the crowd echoed round the stadium. Their first concert in seven years was underway.

The most memorable highlight was the highly publicised appearance of two absolutely gigantic inflatable women on either side of the stage. I had seen a news item where this was shown and wanted to see just how big they were in real life. They were inflated and grew to their full height of sixty feet as *Honky Tonk Women* was played with great gusto by the group. The audience who tended to sing along to all songs were mixing in laughter as these women appeared to reach for the stars. I had to laugh when the brass section about five or six strong were all swaying in time with the music as they played were right at the feet of one of the women. It was the one who had a short skirt, legs crossed, sunglasses and a long cigarette in her mouth. The other had leopard skin shorts and sneakers. They did teeter precariously at times lurching rather than swaying in the night air. The technicians had ropes by which to hopefully control them. I recall thinking that it would be good to just let them float off into the night on the last evening of the tour. Someone would wake up one morning to see a gigantic inflatable woman in their garden.

Jagger had an extra area to run about on – a ramp up towards these "ladies" which he did with his usual aplomb. They did look very tipsy as they were being deflated again. A little redolent of modern British city centres on a Saturday night or holiday resorts like Ibiza and Ayia Napa with its female binge drinking culture. At one point I thought they were going to topple over. The technicians operating them had had plenty of practice as they had toured the USA with these over- sized ladies and there was no mishap.

The second real highlight was the vocal that Merry Clayton had made her own on Gimme Shelter (from the *Let It Bleed* LP), this time performed by Lisa Fischer with great aplomb. "Rape! Murder! It's just a shot away" rang through the night air adding a chilling note to this wonderful song.

103

There is one thing about the parallel World Cup football match that did impinge on the evening, though. There were quite a number of the audience who had small transistor radios with them and they were obviously listening for the score as well as listening and watching The Stones. Not 100% true fans if they could not devote their full attention to the concert.

The result was known by the time the great firework finale brought the concert to a close and the hordes of fans seemed somewhat subdued as they streamed homewards. Normally the atmosphere would remain electric as people told of their favourite bits but Gazza and co had put a bit of a damper on affairs. It may not have gone unnoticed that the final encore song was *(I Can't Get No) Satisfaction*. There is a certain irony in this at the end of a truly great concert.

I didn't know it at the time but this would be the last time that we would see Bill Wyman playing as a Rolling Stone. He had left the group by the time of the next tour four years later.

ST●NES MISCELLANY #6

Wembley Set List:
  Start Me Up
  Sad, Sad, Sad
  Harlem Shuffle
  Tumbling Dice
  Miss You
  Almost Hear You Sigh
  Ruby Tuesday

Rock and a Hard Place
Mixed Emotions
Honky Tonk Women
Midnight Rambler
You Can't Always Get What You Want
Little Red Rooster
Can't Be Seen
Happy
Paint It Black
2000 Light Years from Home
Sympathy for the Devil
Street Fighting Man
Gimme Shelter
It's Only Rock 'n' Roll (But I Like It)
Brown Sugar
Jumpin' Jack Flash
(I Can't Get No) Satisfaction

Alex, my friend and teaching colleague, had accompanied me again but our adventures were much more circumspect this time round. When we reached King's Cross we had found a Kentucky Fried Chicken place open and took our "buckets" back to the train. We did sit in the first class compartments as we had done, before but only till we had finished eating. We had about twenty minutes before the train was due to depart. After tidily placing the empty "buckets" in litter bins on the platform, we went and sat in the regular compartment, which, at close to midnight, was far from full. We were fortunate in that it was not the train that seems to stop at every single station (over twenty) before reaching Huntingdon where my wife was waiting with the car for the drive me back to Stilton and Folksworth for Alex.We headed home

105

with heads still swimming with music after another excellent night out.

Canadian Rumours

▼ MUSIC   CALGARY SUN
12 AUG '94

Stones rumor gathers moss in Banff club

By CLINT REESE and ANIKA VAN WYK
Calgary Sun

BANFF — The Rolling Stones cast a little voodoo magic on the unlikely town of Banff yesterday.

Hundreds of Rolling Stones fans were waiting into the wee hours for the legendary band to rock the town with old friend Colin James.

A rumor the Stones would be making an unscheduled appearance with James — a friend of the band's and sometimes support act — at Banff's Wild Bill's Saloon grew like wildfire yesterday.

"Ralph Klein called looking for tickets, so did Kevin Lowe and Glen Sather," said Wild Bill's bartender Luke Johnston.

At press time, the Stones hadn't appeared but approximately 300 people kept the faith as they lined up outside the saloon.

MICK JAGGER
. . . Banff voodoo

The 400-seat venue has been sold-out for at least a week and only those with pre-purchased tickets were admitted.

James' management company, Mind Over Management, was trying to defuse the rumor.

"We don't know how it started but we've called some radio stations and asked them to stop broadcasting the rumor," said Mind Over Management's Barb McIvor. "An Edmonton radio station refused to stop."

McIvor also said the Calgary office of Virgin Music, the Stones' record label, received at least 40 calls about the possible show.

The Stone's Voodoo Lounge tour included a gig in Indianapolis, Ind., on Wednesday night and they're to play in East Rutherford, N.J., tonight.

We were on holiday in Washington State, USA (Seattle) and then into British Columbia and Alberta, Canada, in the Summer of 1994. We were spending the night in Banff when I chanced upon the local newspaper (reproduced above). The intimation that The Stones were about to play a surprise event locally was being widely talked about. The article claimed that The Stones might be doing a warm up gig to about 400 people. I think that I knew that this was extremely unlikely as they were scheduled to be playing in the neighbouring USA on that same date - but I did dare to hope, even if only for a brief moment, how gaining access might have posed a problem.

Wembley Stadium Concert 15 July 1995

I did see the group about a year later in 1995 at Wembley again on Saturday 15 July this time without Bill Wyman. This was the show that Chris, my son, a current sixth form student, came to with Alex and me. I wanted him to see what I knew would be a great group still on top of their game. We sat in the stand about half way back on the left hand side and, because of the giant screen, we got a great view of everything. I had done the very far away - Hyde Park in 1969 - and the very close - Wembley in 1982 - so this was time for the comfort of a seat about half way back. That is not to say we weren't on our feet a lot of the time singing along and dancing with most of the familiar repertoire.

The Black Crowes provided an excellent support. The influence of the Stones on the band was very evident particularly in songs like *Remedy*. I seem to recall they did a really strong version of *Hard to Handle* – the Otis Redding classic. This was an impressive choice for a support band. Talking of Redding, I still regard his version of *Satisfaction* extremely highly. It is one of those songs that brings out great cover versions. Devo have recorded another fantastic version, too. It shows what a really good song it is.

The Stones' section of the show opened with *Not Fade Away*. There was a very loud rhythmic drumming sound which built slowly into a massive roar and followed by a huge burst of 'dragon' fire which set the mood immediately. It was the first time that I really appreciated that particular song. Buddy Holly would have had difficulty in recognising it. The Stones have been hugely innovative in stage effects copied by others, like U2, but never, in my mind, bettered.

Chris, being young, decided that he wanted to get as close to the stage as he could and, despite my paternal concern that he might not find us again, I gave my approval. He was a big boy now. (Not just grown up but this seventeen-year-old was six foot four tall) He got quite close to the stage and encountered the drummer from The Black Crowes who was in a similar vantage point. Bizarrely, he allowed Chris to sit on his shoulders, to get an even better view. Rock 'n Roll! There was a big screen behind the group on the huge stage that showed video footage during some numbers as well as the traditional close up of the group; Ronnie's slide guitar or Charlie's drumming, for example.

Like many of The Stones' audio-visual extravaganzas, there were some images of a sexual nature edited into the video clips. They were not quite subliminal but if you had blinked you might have missed them. Of course, unlike at home there was no recourse to rewind to check what you thought you had seen. Chris, already showing the signs that would make him so good at his job in TV development recalls a sepia section of film footage which has stuck in his mind. He had never seen Jagger running from side to side of the stage to address his audience more fully and marvelled at the distance that he was obviously travelling. No miming here. It is a testament to his fitness regime that even today after 50 years of performance, he seems almost indefatigable. No one moves quite like Jagger.

ST⬤NES MISCELLANY #7

Wembley Set List:
  Not Fade Away Tumbling Dice
  You Got Me Rocking
  It's All Over Now
  Love Is Strong
  Sparks Will Fly
  Satisfaction
  Beast Of Burden Angie
  Like A Rolling Stone
  Doo Doo Doo Doo (Heartbreaker)
  Gimme Shelter
  I Go Wild Miss You
  Honky Tonk Women
  Before They Make Me Run
  Slipping Away
  Sympathy For The Devil
  Street Fighting Man
  Start Me Up
  It's Only Rock'n' Roll
  Jumpin' Jack Flash

Twickenham Concert 24 August 2003: (Forty Licks)

I have still l got a big card poster from the event (See page 114). I managed to persuade my wife, Sandra, to accompany me to Twickenham - Wembley was being re-developed at that time. It was her first encounter with the group. We had previously been to a number of other rock concerts together seeing The Supremes, The Mark Almond Band, Santana, Bruce Springsteen, Barclay James Harvest, Paul Carrack, Steeleye Span, Tir Na Nog, Ralph McTell, Camel, The Moody Blues, The Blue Jays, Barclay James Harvest,Eric Clapton, Dire Straits, Van Morrison, Michael Jackson, Brian Wilson, BB King and others. You cannot beat live music. Sandra particularly liked Starsailor who were the support act for The Stones.

We sat three seats along from National Theatre of Brent originator Desmond Olivier Dingle. (The actor, Patrick Barlow) He seemed to really enjoy the whole thing, as did everyone in our section. I did keep watching for his reactions I have to admit. You sometimes cannot imagine other people sharing your point of view.

I have always wondered how support acts were chosen. Blues legends would be no problem but you couldn't choose a contemporary rock group of major standing for comparison reasons. The choice of Starsailor was interesting – helping an up and coming band with access to a wider audience or someone who could never steal the show. Starsailor were certainly good. Sandra, as I mentioned, really liked them and their rendition of the hit *Alcoholic* was excellently performed but for me they still lacked that extra bit of charisma. Playing to a half empty arena cannot have helped. I am always amazed just how quickly a place fills up in those final few minutes before a concert starts. About five minutes before The Stones were announced the place seemed only half full. Then, as the group swaggered on to the stage, there was a huge wall of enthusiastic sound. Jagger had been suffering from flu and one show had been cancelled. Some of this might have been relief that he was actually there but more likely the greeting for an old friend. With all apprehension assuaged we could settle in for a rocking two hour treat. There had been no reason to doubt Jagger's voice. Absolutely no hint of a sore throat as he effortlessly went about his business.

The first sound was Keith Richard's familiar guitar riff for *Brown Sugar*. Starting on a high then. The sound was not great for the first three or four numbers and I did begin to wonder whether Twickenham was a good venue. I had been here many times to watch England rugby internationals but once the sound mix was sorted the crowd noise was as ecstatic as if England had scored a push-over try in the last minute to defeat the All Blacks. *Swing Low, Sweet Chariot* has always sounded brilliant there. Biased though I am, I cannot keep listing all of the stand out moments as there were too many. The show was magnificent. The noise of the crowd singing along was deafening. Did they know every single song? As Jagger ran from side to side to greet the audience I wondered if he was covering as much ground as the international players did on a match day. He seemed tireless and worked the crowd by frequent exhortations as he is wont to do..

They had an interlude where they walked down a long catwalk to a small stage around the area of the half way line – the B stage as I have called it in the set list. This was absolutely wonderful. Keith seemed to lap the adulation up the most taking a long time to walk back to the main stage. He had already had his moments when he sang the couple of the songs he is allowed to take the lead vocal on. This always gives Mick a breather and a chance to change his costume.

Both Jagger and Richards announced that this particular venue was like a homecoming for them as they used to play residencies in the early days in neighbouring Richmond.

Sympathy, yet again, as it always seems to be, was a masterpiece as was the encore version of *Jumping Jack Flash* which ended in a crescendo of thundering fireworks. The noise rattled my ribcage and I knew that I had been lucky to see such a consummate show. Sandra, too was impressed. I never thought that I would be able to persuade her to come to a Stones concert. You have to see at least one in your lifetime. Those who pour scorn on the "old wrinklies" are more than likely never to have witnessed a concert in real life the way that people jump on a bandwagon when there is a controversial book or film released and they criticise what they haven't read or seen. The audience, as usual, covered all ages with an obvious bias towards the slightly older generation.

The noise upon leaving the stadium was joyous and everyone seemed to be very happy. Music can be a great "pick me up" at any time.

ST●NES MISCELLANY #8

Set list Twickenham:
Brown Sugar
You Got Me Rocking
Don't Stop
Rocks Off
Wild Horses
You Can't Always Get What You Want

Paint It Black
Tumbling Dice
Slipping Away
Happy Sympathy
For The Devil
Star Star (B-stage)
I Just Want To Make Love To You (B-stage)
Street Fighting Man (B-stage)
Gimme Shelter
Honky Tonk Women
Start Me Up
(I Can't Get No) Satisfaction
Jumping Jack Flash (encore)

The black dots are the holes through which this solid cardboard poster advertising the previous year's best-selling compilation was attached with wire to a lamp post in the car park area. Sandra was not too keen on me liberating it. I wanted to save it in case it rained. We did manage to take it home where it still resides.

I had read about the troubles at the Stones concert in Athens in 1967 ▪there was trouble at a number of those European venues that year - and so, when I saw that they were going to appear in Athens in 2006, I was ready to see a show on foreign soil for the first time. The legendary story of Keith falling out of a palm tree in Fiji, which required him to undergo brain surgery to remove a blood clot, put paid to a number of the allotted dates for European concerts including Athens. They would be rescheduled. I am still waiting for this show to be re-instated. I will recount the events of their triumphant 2018 Manchester Old Trafford Concert later. (See page 175)

Favourite Songs

I will now name my favourite Rolling Stones songs and say why I like them. There are countless lists of peoples' favourite Stones songs and there is a certain obvious familiarity in the songs chosen. I could have done this for their albums but for the most part the top six or seven albums are the same in the lists even if in a slightly different order.

With most groups there is an obvious choice for their best album. *Hotel California* for The Eagles, *Pet Sounds* for The Beach Boys, *Rubber Soul* or *Sgt. Pepper* for The Beatles, *Thriller* or *Off The Wall* for Michael Jackson, *Rumours* for Fleetwood Mac and so on. Yes, these are always subjective but they are widely regarded as their best. With The Rolling Stones, however, there are protagonists for a number of albums *Beggar's Banquet, Let It Bleed, Sticky* Fingers, *Exile On Main Street, Some*

Girls" and latterly, *Blue and Lonesome.* All have their merits for different reasons. The wealth of excellent songs on these albums indicates to me that even though the vast majority were written and produced some time ago, it is, indeed, a good thing that they still endure and resonate in today's world.

Sympathy For The Devil is perhaps the best song ever penned by Jagger and has led to claims of Satanism and Devil Worship. A number of events which followed have been used by critics to help them prove their point. The Altamont Festival being the chief among these. There are those critics of Jagger who still bang on about the link with Lucifer. The truth is the song was embellished by Keith's suggestion of the insistent samba rhythm that underlines the song. Jagger never wrote it in this way but the music is certainly redolent with black magic and voodoo. The lighting for this number in concert and the apparel that Jagger adorns, do make a retrospective devil worship seem feasible even though it certainly is not the case. I am sure that he plays up to this with a certain amount of relish. Jagger has always had certain critics which makes it difficult to appease. John Lydon (aka Johnny Rotten) from the infamous Sex Pistols sang "I am the anti-Christ" in his stinging lyrics to *Anarchy In The UK* but I cannot recall any mention of Devil worship in those heady, punk laden days of the late 1970s. Even his *Belsen is a Gas*, a naturally, highly controversial song, was just regarded as part of the anti-establishment haranguing that the punk movement wallowed in. Lydon, like Jagger before him, is regarded much more favourably today. Age does appear to make a difference.

THE ROLLING STONES: MY TOP TEN SONGS

For a fan like me, choosing just ten Stones' songs has proved to be a very difficult task. As I have already mentioned there are numerous official and unofficial lists of tens, fifties and hundreds of favourite Stones songs. Books, too, have been devoted to it. The Stones longevity and the myriad of songs they have produced means that this is not an easy task. There can never be a definitive list as music, almost by definition, is subjective. The fact is that I actively dislike some of the X Factor style contestants finding their music irrelevant. They are by and large "in it" for the fame and glory and not necessarily the music. But if we all liked the same things just how boring would that be?

Of course I looked at a number of these lists. I wanted to see how high or low my favourites were placed or were they even on the list at all. It was also very useful to remind myself of some almost forgotten gem – a song that might have not normally made my top ten.

In choosing a top ten perhaps just the list ought to suffice. Picking the bones out of a Shakespeare play, for example, for a school exam often means that the joy of the writing can be submerged and lost in the need to study. I do feel, however, that I need to explain the reasons for my Stones songs list and will endeavour to bone pick but hopefully retain the enjoyment factor.

Certain riffs or particular lyrics have a special meaning. One of my very favourite lines in a song comes from the Percy Sledge classic *When A Man Loves A Woman*. The very simple but perceptive line "loving eyes can never see" always gets me. So many of Dylan's lyrics, too, convey great meaning in either their cleverness, humour or sheer brilliance or just the way he articulates it.

"Lily had already taken the dye out of her hair". (*Lily, Rosemary and The Jack of Hearts* from *Blood On The Tracks)* is beautifully delivered.

This is not a delaying tactic but I also feel that it is important to the reader that I just list some of my very favourite non Rolling Stones songs as a context for the detailed list to follow. Knowing some of the music that I like should help an understanding of my choices. I do have to say that my all-time top ten non Stones songs does frequently change and I could easily make it a top forty.... but worry not, I won't.

In no particular order:
Howlin' Wolf – *Smokestack Lightning*; Santana – *I'll Be Waiting*; Ry Cooder (with Harry Dean Stanton)- *Across The Borderline;* Sandy Denny – *Who Knows Where The Time Goes?;* Neil Young – *Keep On Rocking In The Free World, Like A Hurricane*"; Dire Straits-*On Every Street;* Mark Knopfler – *Sailing To Philadelphia;* Bill Callahan –*Tom Cain;* The Who – *Won't Get Fooled Again*; Metallica – *Nothing Else Matters*; Bob Dylan – *Lily, Rosemary & The Jack Of Hearts, Sara*; Red Hot Chili Peppers –*Californication*; The Tea Party –*In This Time.*

Here goes then......
I earlier gave examples of songs from the different genres of music put out by The Rolling Stones. Jim Beviglia's book "Counting Down the Rolling Stones. Their 100 Finest Songs" alludes to these different styles and says that The Stones were "so damn good at them". Writing about such a range of styles in a critique of *I Got The Blues* from *Sticky Fingers*, Jim Beviglia states that "there

was sad country (*Wild Horses*), rambling country (*Dead Flowers*), grooving rock (*Bitch*), boogie rock (*Brown Sugar*), and, maybe regrettably, jam rock (*Can't You Hear Me Knocking*) and, of course, the blues (*You Gotta Move*)." Beviglia goes on to say - and this is one of the reasons I so love their music - "These were not mere homages. This was a band so fluent in the respective styles and yet so confident in their own musical personality that their identity shined through the material even as they displayed stunning versatility". Beviglia actually fails to identify one further genre on *Sticky Fingers*. The closing song *Moonlight Mile* is admittedly difficult to categorize with its oriental overtones and sweeping strings but, as you will see (below) a majestic performance from the group. And, by the way, Jim, there is nothing wrong with jam rock when it is played well.

My list of contenders (in no particular order)

Satisfaction, Brown Sugar, Jumpin Jack Flash, Paint It Black, Money, Beast Of Burden, Wild Horses, Moonlight Mile, Time Waits for No One, Star Star, Gimme Shelter, Around and Around, Far Away Eyes, Play With Fire, Rough Justice, Honky Tonk Women, Sympathy For The Devil, Street Fighting Man, Under My Thumb, Tumblin' Dice, 19th Nervous Breakdown, Start Me Up, Just My Imagination, Everybody Needs Somebody, Mixed Emotions, Ride 'em On Down.

Time Waits For No One

It is one of those tracks that when you play it you have to repeat the process several/many times over. It is such a mesmeric track right from the metronomic beat at the very start. It is like a ticking clock. I won't say that it hypnotises you into liking it but it is very addictive and continues through to the very end of the track. While Watts and Wyman lay down a jazz style beat, it is the wonderfully eccentric Ray Cooper who provides the tambourine and maracas for the insistent beat. Looking at concert set lists that show you just how many times each Stones track has been played, you discover that this is ONE song that they have never EVER played at any concert. It has, also, only appeared in two compilations *Sucking in the Seventies* (1981). The track also appeared on the earlier British compilation album *Time Waits for No One: Anthology 1971–1977*, issued in 1979 but only on vinyl, It is such a deliciously mellifluous piece of music that this beggars belief.

I can understand, however, why they haven't played it since Taylor's departure. It is his song. To discover that there is no record of live footage by The Rolling Stones on YouTube, nor any record of it ever being performed live, is astonishing and very disappointing.

I had hoped that when Mick Taylor re-joined the group for their 50th anniversary gigs that it might get an airing but, alas, no. This is the song that it is sometimes reputed to be the final breaking point for Taylor and triggering his departure from the group. He received absolutely no recognition for his contribution to the writing of this song. It clearly has his stamp all over it. He had recently been in Brazil and the South American influence in the guitar work is clearly evident. Carlos Santana would have been proud to have come up with this melody. Taylor's extended outro to this song proves to be his swansong as he leaves the group shortly after this... but what a soaring, shimmering way to bid farewell. The piano playing, too, (always an important aspect in Stones' music be it Ian Stewart, Nicky Hopkins, Billy Preston or the current Chuck Leavell) adds another level to the climax of this song. The swirling runs are this time provided by Hopkins' piano and are the perfect foil to Taylor's exquisite guitar. You can find this song on YouTube but only by Taylor as a solo artist. The Stones version is sadly an audio one only. I love to play this track to people who think that the Stones are a one trick pony as far as music is concerned. It falls into the same category as *Moonlight Mile* and *Winter,* as we will see. The cleverness of Jagger's lyrics are surely undeniable here. The irony of "Time waits for no one, and it won't wait for me" becomes more apparent the longer the group stay together. Jagger does not preclude himself either from those who time has in its sights. The very early "Time is on my side, Yes it is" (1964) seems to have been overtaken by reality.

"Yes, star crossed in pleasure the stream flows on by Yes, as we're sated in leisure, we watch it fly"

The lyrics to this song are almost anachronistic in style. Certainly not Keats or Shelley, but a very formal way of phrasing words "no favours has he" for example, and:

"Men, they build towers to their passing yes, to their fame everlasting/Here he comes chopping and reaping, hear him laughing at their cheating"

If not my all-time favourite track it is certainly very close and still regularly played by me.

Moonlight Mile
I made reference to this song in the previous part, so I will deal with it next. It is another with one of those delicious Taylor guitar pieces. This is a magnificent studio

production from start to finish featuring an overlay of strings from the maestro of this genre, Paul Buckmaster. Elton John's *Madman Across The Water* album has tracks with a similar Buckmaster contribution (it's another album I rate highly). Coupled with Charlie's exemplary use of cymbals the overall feel of this song is undeniably oriental. I like the restrained, almost weary nature of the song. The piano is similarly restrained and poignant, too. The song has often been likened to a film score such is its grandness. My understanding is that Keith is not on this recording at all even though, as usual, he gets a writing credit with Jagger. Taylor's 12 string playing is given absolute full rein.

This song is another underappreciated Stones classic. In a review of this song, Bill Janovitz (allmusic- and best-known as the guitarist and lead singer with Buffalo Tom) says, "Though the song still referenced drugs and the road life of a pop-music celebrity, it really is a rare example of Jagger letting go of his public persona, offering a behind-the-scenes glimpse of the weariness that accompanies the pressures of keeping up appearances as a sex-drugs-and-rock & roll star". The lyric is certainly melancholic reflecting the hard grind of life on the road. Will he make home it to be with his love? You are really drawn into the song.

"I am just living to be lying by your side/but I am just about a moonlight mile on down the road"

He is certainly seeking some form of peace despite the wind, rain and snow of the storm.

The line "In the window there's a face you know" conjures up different interpretations. Is it a window back home where someone waits for him, or is it a window in the train he is travelling in, with the image of a loved one or even himself reflected in the darkened glass as he wearily contemplates returning home? This is Jagger with his guard down and vulnerable.

I have always been intrigued by the line "With a head full of snow". It is easy to find things in lyrics that were never intended but this possible cocaine reference could also hint at another hindrance in getting home. Jagger later refuted this as a drug reference but then, he would, wouldn't he?

Certainly one of the very best atmospheric and exotic songs the Stones ever recorded. There are some similarities to the song *Winter* from *Goat's Head Soup* – Buckmaster strings and impeccable Taylor guitar again in Keith's absence from the recording. Jim Price, usually a key part of the brass section on trumpet, plays piano on the track.

This song is best played late at night. I often listen with headphones on and in the dark. The emotional insight into life on the road comes through brilliantly. The final minute and a half is a wondrously, shimmering instrumental with the guitar and piano to the fore. Turn it up loud.

Those who only know the group through the myriad of hit singles may have missed this brilliant album cut from *Sticky Fingers*. Shame on you. Give it a listen.

(I Can't Get No) Satisfaction
You can't be a fan 'cause you don't like/ the same kinda music as me. (With immense apologies to Mick Jagger). Regardless of that instantly identifiable opening

riff, this song has a lyric that shouted out to me as an eighteen year old young man in 1965, the things I wanted to hear. I loved the anti-Big Brother, anti-advertising aspect of it. Be an individual. The failure to connect with the opposite sex as epitomised by the title rang true, too. The riff is one that anyone who has picked up a guitar can play rather like *Smoke on the Water*. This does not make you a guitar player however – certainly not me. The best riffs are the simplest ones. A few, well ordered, notes are all that is required – that and the much more difficult ability to think of it in the first place. The guitar riff does remind me of the horn arrangement from Martha & the Vandellas' classic *Nowhere to Run*. This cannot be regarded as a bad thing. The full title of the song – the 'I Can't Get No' bit is a grammatical contradiction – a double negative and, believe it or not, the song was criticised in some quarters for this very fact upon release. My wife often chides me when I see apostrophes in plurals or misspellings on TV, with the phrase "Put your red pen away". As a retired teacher I find that I cannot. It does irk me that such mistakes are made. However, in this song, the double negative works well. It is not a grammatical mistake. The title echoes the contradictions in life between what we want and can't get and what we get and say we don't want. Whatever the truth behind Keith's falling asleep with his tape recorder still running and managing to record probably the greatest riff in rock n roll history before recording a tape full of snoring, this song was one of the very first to have an intelligent lyric in my eyes. (I didn't appreciate Bob Dylan properly for another year or so).

"When I'm watchin' my TV
And that man comes on to tell me

How white my shirts can be
But he can't be a man 'cause he doesn't smoke
The same cigarettes as me"

Charlie Watts' simple, yet utterly appropriate, back-beat before the "Hey! Hey! Hey!" in the chorus is another vital component of this song. Whenever I hear this played now at a party or wedding reception, everyone seems to know the words and sings along at full tilt. *Satisfaction* has been described as the best Rock song ever written by a number of important critics. It is therefore very difficult for me to dispute that. It has stood the test of time. It was regarded as an instant classic in 1965 commenting on the polar forces that powered it then. It is no less powerful today - over 50 years later – its message still resonating loudly whenever it is played. The song ends with "'cause you see I'm on a losing streak" which might refer to the character in the song but most certainly not to one of the very finest Jagger Richards compositions. It was only a winning streak from here especially in the USA.

Beast Of Burden

It is important to know the background to this song. Ronnie Wood had just established himself as a full member of the group and Keith Richards was at a crossroads in that his dalliance with heroin had meant him not taking a full part in the group. It is ironic to think that this was the criticism that Mick and Keith had levelled at Brian Jones not that many years before. According to the Stones fan site *Time Is On Our Side*, while *Burden* was largely written by Jagger, the song started with Richards, who is quoted as saying "All I did was throw out the phrase 'beast of burden' to Mick, and I played him the music, and then he took it off by himself and did a

124

beautiful job on it". Richards is purportedly trying to apologise for his absences due to drugs and legal issues while acknowledging that Jagger had been carrying the running of the band. Keith was asking to be allowed to share the weight again.

In the liner notes to the 1993 compilation *Jump Back*, Jagger says, "Lyrically, this wasn't particularly heartfelt in a personal way. It's a soul begging song, an attitude song. It was one of those where you get one melodic lick, break it down and work it up; there are two parts here which are basically the same". For me Keith's melodic lick works really well. There are some great versions of this song which shows that the basic material is more than just the sound. Bette Midler (Check out the YouTube version with Jagger guesting) and Semon 'Tiny' Holmes from a wonderful covers album called *Paint It Blue* which I bought from a great little record shop in Greenwich Village, New York, featuring a wealth of blues artists and treatments of Stones songs, are two which instantly spring to mind. I mentioned Charlie's drumming in *Satisfaction* as being an integral part of the success of the sound; in *Beast of Burden* his insistent beat sets the tone for a joyous overall piece of music. The famed duelling of the two guitars interweaving are very evident on this record. Characteristically, Richards and Wood trade off rolling, fluid licks. Neither is really playing lead or rhythm guitar, they both slip in and out, one playing high while the other is low. As Richards is often wont to say sometimes they don't even know who is playing which part. I do find this a little hard to comprehend. It suggests an auto pilot style of playing which I can't quite subscribe to. Whatever... it works. A recent re-issue of *Some Girls* and with a DVD of a concert in Texas at that time has brought this song back into prominence again and richly deserved. The Stones had been accused of being no longer valid. This album shows palpably that this is an unworthy criticism.   Jagger's vocal, sad, pleading and defiant, makes reference to an unexpected vulnerability "Ain't I rough enough? Ain't I tough enough? Ain't I rich enough?"

Ultimate Classic Rock Magazine January 2013 writes this about the song: "As well as it works as an anthem of honest regret and brotherly love, *Beast of Burden* is also a pretty terrific admission of intrinsic need — and a defiant expression of strength — which, along with its gently strutting beat and fluidly intertwining lead guitars, helped make the song a Top 10 U.S. hit in late 1978. It also boasts more than a few lines that go perfectly with that Friday evening drive out of the company parking lot, but why wait for 5 o'clock? Hit the 'play' button… turn up the volume, and let the weekend start now."

I could not agree more.

Star Star

The song was originally titled *Starfucker* until Atlantic Records owner Ahmet Ertegün (Atlantic was the distributor of Rolling Stones Records) insisted on the change. I cannot think why!! I know that I shouldn't like this song because of the lyrics but it is one of those with an infectious riff that I find difficult to ignore.

The song gained notoriety not only for explicit lyrics alluding to sex acts involving fruit (among other things): "Your tricks with fruit was kind a cute, I bet you keep your pussy clean" but also for controversial mentions of such celebrities as John Wayne and Steve McQueen. Deliberate controversy here again.

"Yeah, Ali McGraw got mad with you
For givin' head to Steve McQueen"

It was released about nine months after Carly Simon's affair with Jagger and the release of the song, *You're So Vain*. Simon, who was by now married to fellow singer-songwriter James Taylor, had moved to Hollywood, which is mentioned in the lyrics of *Star Star*. While discussing the song, the band members have always referred to the song by its original title. A live performance was captured and released on 1977's *Love You Live*. (Atlantic also tinkered with the mix, drowning a few key words with studio trickery, on all pressings except the very first promo copies.)

Star Star for me is a classic Chuck Berry style rocker that slowly increases in momentum as the song progresses. (Having the DVD copy of *Hail, Hail Rock 'n' Roll* in which Keith plays with his hero Chuck Berry, I always recall the bit where Berry seriously chides Richards about the way he is not properly bending the strings in trying to imitate the master on *Carol*. It always makes me laugh.). The opening lick, stabs in the verses and solo are played by Keith Richards and the rhythm guitar by Mick Taylor. Bill Wyman's bass line doesn't start until the second verse just as Jagger is singing "Honey, honey" in that slightly drawled American way he employs a lot, that I always have to sing along to, whenever I hear the song. I am sure this would have been a major hit if it had been played on the radio at the time. That, in reality, was never going to happen. It was never going to feature on *Top Of The Pops*. It was never going to feature anywhere. MTV was many years away especially the European version.

Gimme Shelter

Any song which carries the lines: "Rape, murder! It's just a shot away" and opens with "Oh, a storm is threat'ning my very life today" has to be taken seriously. This stand out classic Stones song will, unfortunately, always be associated with the death of Meredith Hunter at Altamont being performed, prophetically, minutes before his death. Many observers of the sixties hippie scene claim that this song and that event brought a dramatic closure to that era - an end to the peace and love ethic that epitomised the Woodstock Festival from earlier in that year. The war in Viet Nam had escalated by this time, too, and provided an apposite backdrop to the song. This war was a really nasty war with the violence being portrayed on TV screens every night. It was a a war which the people, in general, objected to. Jagger in an interview with *Rolling Stone* magazine described the track *Gimme Shelter* as "a kind of end of the world song. It's apocalypse. The whole *Let It Bleed* album is like that". The energy and sensuality of the Stones shines brightly throughout the song right from the first piano chord. Keith's spidery guitar intro collapses into deep rumble with Charlie's drums pounding away around Jagger's bluesy howl and banshee gospel of the marvellous Merry Clayton. Her extraordinary powerful, backing vocals virtually steal the song away from Jagger. Her performance on the song where she was summoned from her bed may have contributed to the miscarriage she suffered very shortly afterwards. Her chilling vocals articulated at full tilt and the fact that the studio had a very heavy door to negotiate have been mentioned in this context. I have seen the wondrous Lisa Fisher sing this several times and you are never aware that she is a just a backing singer. The harmonies are just spot on, too. It is an excellently crafted

song with Charlie's rhythmic drumming carrying the song along. Jagger's harp playing, too, is chilling. When one talks of pop music, this epic composition far transcends that term. This is serious music with a capital 'S'. Coupled with the equally dark *Midnight Rambler* written at about the same time, those who criticised the Stones for their occult dabblings maybe had a point. *I Want To Hold Your Hand* it certainly ain't! The unrelenting lyrics conjure up a dystopian world, Martin Scorsese has used the song in three of his films *Casino, Goodfellas"* and *The Departed.* (See the Martin Scorsese section page 145). It has also been used in a number of TV shows and the video game *Call of Duty: Black Ops.*
"Ooh, see the fire is sweepin'
Our very street today
Burns like a red coal carpet
Mad bull lost your way"

The "Rape, murder! It's just a shot away" line is repeated several times as the song draws to a close, followed by "War, children It's just a shot away." Then we get the dark admission "Love, sisters, it's just a kiss away," Jagger softly amends, but the kiss didn't come, the shelter wasn't found. This chilling song is deservedly reserved for the encore slot of the Stone's concert performances. A timeless masterpiece and still appropriate for American society today. In *Gimme Shelter* all aspects of the song seem to marry perfectly from Richards intense guitar riff to the overwhelming beauty of Mary Clayton's backing vocals that sends shivers down the spine.

Wild Horses
Wild Horses is one of those songs that has gathered momentum over the years with a myriad of artists

covering it. I almost like the Susan Boyle version (but do not tell anyone!).

I imagine that her recording of it, was, for many people, the very first time that they were aware of this song or that it was a Stones song. The influence of Gram Parsons is quite clear in the writing and the music. He hung out with the Stones during their French exile. Some claim that he even wrote or co-wrote the song about his sister Avis. He was certainly even given permission by Jagger and Richards to release it with his Flying Burrito Brothers group before The Stones did. It is a very sentimental song with Parson's country feel clearly present. It is far removed from the traditional Rolling Stones song. What gives it added poignancy is that Richards claims to have written the chorus to his infant son before embarking on the 1969 tour of the USA and it is sometimes even rumoured that Jagger's lyrics could reflect the broken romance with Marianne though this was well over by then.

"I watched you suffer a dull aching pain
Now you decided to show me the same
No sweeping exits or offstage lines
Could make me feel bitter or treat you unkind
Wild horses couldn't drag me away"

Whoever it is about, there is no denying that it is a very emotional song. The bittersweet lyrics are both tender, wistful and certainly vulnerable. The interweaving of acoustic guitar parts by Richards and Taylor make it a stand out track from one of their best albums *Sticky Fingers*. Richards uses a 12 string guitar which helps to create the melancholy in his playing. The harmony of the chorus between Jagger and Richards is pure country and pure magic. Charlie again, this time with brushes, gives the song body. I often wonder how Americans feel about

British singers affecting an American accent for their songs. (We do owe them payback for those who try cockney accents? – Thank you, and good night Dick Van Dyke).

Jagger does this on many Stones songs to good effect perhaps none better than on the *The Girl With The Faraway Eyes*. *Wild Horses* has deservedly earned its place as a country standard. Whoever would have thought of Rolling Stones songs becoming standards?

There is a music duo called the Dead Beatles based in Kalamata, Greece, near where I live. (John, who is English and Giorgos, who is Greek). They play cover versions very competently. I have seen them a couple of times. I visited their Facebook page and suggested that they learned to play *Wild Horses* as it seemed to suit their guitar and vocal style very well. When I saw them next there was no reference to any of The Rolling Stones catalogue. At the end of the gig we were just about to get up to leave when John announced "This one is for Mike" and they launched into a really good version of the song. Of course I went up to them after the gig to congratulate and thank them.

Sympathy For The Devil
An ironic song performed by Jagger as the Devil presiding over a number of famous and infamous world events. These events are from the point of view of the Devil himself. Famously, Jagger had to change the line "Who killed Kennedy" to a plural when JFK's brother, Robert, was also assassinated. The original line was perhaps a touch lazy but the addition of the Robert Kennedy assassination makes it much more powerful. I have seen reference to the fact that adding this new line at the last

moment could have been shock mongering, if there is such a word, but I feel that it makes it much stronger and evocative.

"Pleased to meet you
Hope you guess my name
But what's puzzling you
Is the nature of my game"

The song is mainly the work of Jagger who originally wrote it as a Dylanesque folk song. Keith persuaded Mick to change it to a samba driven piece with a hypnotic groove accompanied by additional primitive percussion. (See the 1969 Hyde Park Concert version). The tribal samba sound easily conjures up images of black magic or voodoo, especially if you allow it to! Those tribal drums open the piece and continue their unrelenting beat followed by the woo woos. Apart from these woo woos that are ever present, a hypnotic feel is created by the constant tempo of the music. It does not change pace. The music itself is quite sinister matching the lyric very well. It is hypnotic, disturbing, unsettling and provocative. It is a truly grown-up song with excellent imagery. Who could imagine a song about the Devil wondering what people think about him?

Reference to Christ and the crucifixion, the Communist take- over in Russia, Nazi tanks sweeping through Europe and the assassination of a US President and his brother form the heart of this song. Jagger always seems to dress up when performing this in concert with a variety of capes. Those ready to attack Jagger, preferred to accuse him of Satanism rather than being an excellent writer, and overlooking the influence of Baudelaire and

Bulgakov on this former university student. The Bay City Rollers it aint!

Sympathy is based on Bulgakov's novel *The Master and Margarita*, and like the novel highlights one corrupt establishment being overthrown only to become corrupt. This forms a cycle which mechanically repeats itself like the flip of a coin – the fatalistic *as heads is tails* (of the song) philosophy. One such interpretation of this song would be – 'new boss, same as the old boss'.

When Jagger sings:
"Just as every cop is a criminal
and all the sinners saints
As heads is tails, just call me Lucifer
Cause I'm in need of some restraint".
It is certainly genuinely spooky. His vocal is uncompromising. "Far Out" magazine described it as coming from " the pits of Hell". It is a song that makes you listen to what he is going to refer to next and certainly encapsulating key events in history.

The song was originally called *The Devil Is My Name*. It never harmed record sales to have this notoriety. Musicians and artists had played with devilry before but for pop music this was something else. Jagger WAS the Devil! Richards told *Rolling Stone*: "Before, we were just innocent kids out for a good time." But after *Sympathy For The Devil*, he said, "they're saying, 'They're evil, they're evil'. Of course they were not but as far as image goes this was really helpful.

On a trivial note I watched a Will Smith film *Focus* in which the number of woo woos in the song was a featured part of a betting scenario. It works out at 124. When I saw

The Stones live in Manchester in 2018 I actually counted them and made it a much higher total. My brother Paul, who had accompanied me, was less than impressed with my attention to detail when I revealed this. He had just been enjoying the performance.

Seriously though, this is a very intelligently crafted song written at a time when Jagger's talent was at its peak. A lot of the dross that exists today in the pop world is shown to be just that in comparison to this articulate, yet disturbing, masterpiece. The song certainly helps to set the seal on the way the end of the decade was heading.

When he sings "Please allow me to introduce myself, I'm a man of wealth and taste", those who wanted to believe that Jagger was Lucifer in reality could easily do so. The feeling that The Stones were the embodiment of evil and dabbling in black magic was acknowledged by Richards in his book *Life*. Of course, this was not true, though the events of the ill-fated Altamont concert of 1969 were open to different interpretations.

The unfortunate Meredith Hunter was stabbed to death at the concert. Bad reporting claimed it was during "Sympathy". The trouble had started during that song but he was murdered some several songs later. If some elements of the press wanted to make a case out of misguided or malevolent reporting then there was little that could be done. The Stones reputation for evil was there for anyone to behold. The reality was that this reputation for devil worship was merely cosmetic. After a scathing attack by Rolling Stone magazine, when they were accused of "diabolical egotism", the group did not play the song live again for several years. Surely real-life Satanists would have played it again and again. Today it is always one of the standout songs in any Stones concert set list. Testament to its literary prowess and powerful imagery.

Paint It Black

In the late 1980s, *Paint It Black* became associated with the Viet Nam War due to its use in both the ending credits of the 1987 Stanley Kubrick film, *Full Metal Jacket* and its use as the theme song for *Tour Of Duty*, a CBS-TV show about the Viet Nam war which ran from 1987-1990. Following in the wake of the very successful Oliver Stone movie *Platoon, Tour of Duty* was the first series on TV to portray this war. The airing of the song on the TV show, which played around the world, contributed to its revised popularity in the late 1980s-early-1990s. Later marketing and packaging of the song in those years also referred to the *Tour of Duty* TV show. The show was shown in the UK on ITV and I used to watch it even though it was usually given a very late night slot. It would often start at midnight.

Having written my History thesis on Ho Chi Minh and always been interested in the Viet Nam War(s), I, too, have come to associate the song with this conflict.

On the songfacts.com website a Viet Nam veteran, "Bill", made the following observation about the association of *Paint It Black* and the Viet Nam War:

"…While The Rolling Stones' song *Paint It Black* was not written about the Viet Nam War, it has great meaning for many combat veterans from that war. The depression, the aura of premature death, loss of innocence, abandonment of all hope are perfectly expressed in the song. When you walk off the killing fields, still alive, physically intact, you want everything painted black, like your heart, your soul, you mind, your life."

This shows the impact that music can have at particular times in one's life. Not quite the "Listen, they are playing our song, darling" scenario but something much more powerful and meaningful. There are many Stones songs that hold this association for me.

Like a number of Rolling Stones songs the intro is sublime. The opening sitar followed by the stomping sound of Watt's drums with Jagger's snarling lyric make this record a stand out track. He almost spits the words out in his anger. It has become one of the very most favourite tracks for many fans. It is a very bleak and depressing picture that is painted (pun intended). The line "I have to turn my head until my darkness goes" is often said to have come from the James Joyce intellectual masterpiece, *Ulysses,* and may have served as inspiration for Jagger. Whether this is true or not Jagger was not averse to using literature as source material for his lyrics.

"Maybe then I'll fade away and not have to face the facts, It's not easy facing up when your whole world is black".

I have referred to a dystopian world in other songs and the whole mood is certainly black as the song title suggests.

The opening line "I see a red door and I want it painted black" I once saw described as a Fascist victory over Communism which only serves to show that any lyric can be interpreted in many different ways and often completely wrongly. The beauty of lyric interpretation is usually that there is never any wrong answer unless the writer has actually expressed the meaning elsewhere.

Another plausible theory, and one with which I have a strong empathy, is that it is about a lover who has died and the reference to "a line of cars and they're all painted black" represents a hearse and the following procession of limos. The line "With flowers and my love both never to come back" is about the flowers from the funeral and her in the hearse. This would certainly explain the anger and the depression demonstrated by the singer.

This song was originally called P*aint It, Black* but the record company missed out the punctuation. The first number one record in the UK to feature a sitar and a grammatical error.

Brian Jones scarcely gets good press but his skill as a multi-instrumentalist was certainly to the fore with the sitar introduction on this record. The dulcimer was featured on *I Am Waiting* while the mellotron and the theremin are played by him on *2,000 Light Years From Home*. On *She's A Rainbow*, it is his fingers that nimbly play the trumpet part. The recorder is effectively utilised on *Ruby Tuesday* and, finally, how cool is his playing of the marimba on *Under My Thumb*? His thirst for experimentation for new sonic textures was well known. His expertise was well lauded. What a shame, then, that he allowed the drugs to dominate his life. We can only sadly surmise what he might have achieved.

Start Me Up

This song was originally written as a reggae song from the *Black & Blue* era but not released in its changed form till the *Tattoo You* album of 1981. It is an oft played track by all sorts of events and organisations. Teresa May, as the newly elected leader of the Conservative Party marched on to the conference stage to it at the Party Conference in October 2016. I am not sure that she had ever listened to the whole song as the words "You make a dead man cum" did not seem wholly appropriate.

The possible double entendre nature of the lyric are not difficult to spot:

"If you like it you can slide it up, slide it up
Don't make a grown man cry
My eyes dilate, my lips go green
My hands are greasy
She's a mean, mean machine"

It has an instantly recognisable Keith riff featuring a strong Charlie Watts back beat and an echoing bass line from Bill Wyman that sets the tone for the song. The video of this song looks like a Jane Fonda workout and has an infectious, stomping beat throughout. The lyric contains very thinly disguised sexual references (so what's new?) and is delivered with gusto from Jagger. No wonder they have often chosen to open their concert performances with it.

My personal involvement with this song concerns a trip with my sister Barbara, and her husband, Carl, along with his son Simon and our son Chris. We motored to Rospico in Brittany with Carl in the driver's seat. I had provided a music cassette for the journey which heavily featured Rolling Stones tracks. Some good drive time music guaranteed. On the journey on the other side of the Channel, we stopped for a rest and some coffee. I turned the cassette in the car over and the first track on the other side was *Start Me Up*. Sandra, who had probably had enough music by then shouted out in a very slow and dramatic fashion: "Turn that off, now!". The rest of us started to laugh and even Sandra joined in when she realised how she had sounded. To this day whenever that track is playing, we have to say "Turn that off, now" and, of course, we don't.

Jumpin' Jack Flash

Famously inspired by the Redlands gardener Jack Dyer who is said to have woken Jagger up while working and prompting him to ask Keith who he was. Richards told him it was Jumping Jack and the song was born from this chance phrase...or, at least, that is the story. Another story is that Bill Wyman (from his book *Stone Alone)* came up with the distinctive riff on keyboards but never got any credit for it. Keith now claims it is his favourite guitar riff. Whoever devised the riff, it is certainly one of the very best. Keith's dalliance with open D blues tuning produces dynamic results. "Q" magazine in 2005 put the song at number two in its all-time guitar tracks. However, it evolved, it is one of the very best Stones songs. It was written after the Satanic Majesties album and widely regarded as a return to their blues rock best after their brief psychedelic sojourn away.

Right from the opening "Watch it!" we are drawn into some powerful imagery – crossfire hurricanes, toothless hags, straps across the back, crowned with a spike right through the head and so on. The slightly comforting "But it's all right now, in fact it's a gas" attempts to reassures the listener. It is OK – he is Jumpin' Jack Flash. I love the way Jagger almost spits the words out and the very strident way that the music is played. Wyman's bass again throbbing loudly and insistently. The jangly guitar sound is almost like the swirl of bagpipes throughout and especially at the end where the sound of the organ inter-weaves with the snarling guitars as the line "Jumpin' Jack Flash, it's a gas, gas, gas" is repeated over and over into the fade. I remember that I always used to turn that bit up when listening to the song and my mother invariably asked me to turn it down. I think she would have preferred "off" rather than "down". The fading guitars at the close of the song have always reminded me those bag-pipes I mentioned and it is this that made me turn the sound up. I just love that sound.

The accompanying video was very imposing, too. Mi-chael Lindsay-Hogg, who had cut his teeth on *Ready Steady Go*, made the promotional video. Jagger, with some sort of tribal war paint on his face, Jones, with a massive fake tan and huge plastic sunglasses, Richards, looking cool in his shades, Charlie, looking intense and finally the haunting look of Bill Wyman almost oblivious to the camera. The whole video was shot in a dark room adding to the aggressive imagery. This heightened my love of the song a whole decade before pop videos were to be the norm with the birth of MTV.

Talking of film, the song has a famous link with the Scorsese film *Mean Streets* where De Niro walks in slow-motion to a bar and the line "I was born in a crossfire hurricane" immediately sums up his character.

I was about to critique *Brown Sugar* when I counted up and saw that I had already written about eleven songs for my top ten. Rather than either cut one of the previous ones or add a twelfth I decided to leave it as it is....my top eleven. Not sure that it will catch on. The lyrics of this controversial song are, however, discussed earlier in this book, in a different context, as you should have already have discovered. (See pages 27 - 30).

Blue Roots CD

This is a picture of the *Blue Roots* CD that I compiled and sent to Mick Jagger for his consideration. I was seeking no reward but felt that as the group had committed to disc a solid body of Blues recordings already, that they ought to release a pure Blues album. This was a long way before the *Blue and Lonesome* disc which has performed so well and was so wonderfully received, having been recorded in just three days if reports are accurate. I had discovered that although he and Jerry Hall had split up he was living in the house next door so I was able to work out where to send the disc. Needless to say he never replied. I expect that some security person dealt with a suspicious package before it reached him. It was meant as a creative suggestion only. That's what I tell myself!

Blue Roots is an album that is culled from a number of Rolling Stones recordings from their first LP to later CDs. Importantly, too, it contains tracks that The Stones have individually, or in smaller cohorts, recorded with various bluesmen on other albums.

Since those early days when they invited "forgotten" or ignored blues legends to guest on their tours, it has been impossible to discount the tremendous influence that the blues has played in their music.

These timeless tracks trace the lifeblood of The Rolling Stones. I have added a bonus track that shows the compliment has been reciprocated. The Junior Wells version of *Satisfaction* is given the full blown treatment so that it sounds like a blues classic. Testament indeed.

Blue Roots Track listing/credits

Little Red Rooster   Willie Dixon *
Don't Start Me to Talkin' Sonny Boy Williamson **
I Can't Be Satisfied McKinley Morganfield (Muddy Waters)
Little Baby Willie Dixon*
I Just Wanna Make Love To You Willie Dixon*
Crawlin' King Snake John Lee Hooker ***
Paying The Cost To Be Boss BB King ****
You Gotta Move Fred McDowell*
It Hurts Me Too Elmore James *****
Shake Your Hips James Moore (Slim Harpo)*
I Can't Stand It Elias McDaniel Bo Diddley)/ Ron Wood
Ventilator Blues Jagger/Taylor/Richards*
Love In Vain Trad arranged/new words Jagger/ Richards*
Goin'Away Baby   Jimmy Rogers **
Bye Bye Johnnie Chuck Berry*
Satisfaction   Jagger/Richards +

Performed by
 The Rolling Stones *
Jimmy Rogers with The Rolling Stones **
 John Lee Hooker with Keith ***
 BB King with the Rolling Stones ****
Mick Bill Charlie with Nicky Hopkins and Ry Cooder *****
Junior Wells featuring Bob Margolin

143

Martin Scorsese's Use of The Rolling Stones

Martin Scorsese, who made the renowned rockumentary/drama *Shine A Light* (2008) about The Rolling Stones, has used songs from the band on numerous occasions. Somehow, their music seems to make the perfect backdrop to murder, chaos or an introduction to a menacing character.

"There is a drive and authority to their music and also an edge to it," Martin Scorsese explains in notes for *Shine a Light*. The following is a list of films that feature the songs. I include this because, to me, it adds authority to the Rolling Stones canon of work when such a prestigious film maker decides to employ their music to help build the mood of a particular scene. *Gimme Shelter* actually features three times in his mafia films. There is, therefore, no mistaking his personal favourite Stones song.

ST●NES MISCELLANY #9

MEAN STREETS (1973) - *Jumpin' Jack Flash*: Meet crazy Robert De Niro as he saunters in slow motion, a woman on each arm, into a Little Italy bar. *Tell Me*: Meet conflicted mobster Harvey Keitel as he boogies into a strip club and has a drink.

GOODFELLAS (1990) - *Gimme Shelter*: Against the mob boss's orders, Ray Liotta starts dealing cocaine. *Monkey Man*: Liotta juggles his family, girlfriend and lots of cocaine. Encore: He and wife Lorraine Bracco stash guns in hermother's garbage can. *Memo From Turner*: Liotta thinks that police helicopters are following him.

CASINO (1995) - *Can't You Hear Me Knocking*: Mob man Joe Pesci sets up his Vegas burglary ring. *Gimme*

Shelter: Pesci, again, getting mixed up in a string of murders. Encore: Cops shoot a thug. *"Heart of Stone*: Casino boss Robert De Niro falls for sexy hustler Sharon Stone. *Long Long While*: Pesci grabs a pen and jabs a jerk in the jugular. (*I Can't Get No) Satisfaction:* (A Devo cover version and terrific fun. Check out the video.) De Niro gets really mad at his adulterous, druggie wife. *Sweet Virginia*: De Niro ejects a cowboy slob from his casino.

THE DEPARTED (2006) - *Gimme Shelter*: Meet mob boss Jack Nicholson: "No one gives it to you. You have to take it." *Let It Loose*: Nicholson welcomes Leonardo Di Caprio - an undercover cop - by smashing his broken arm.

A final link and major link between Scorsese and particularly Jagger (so far) is the TV series *VINYL* about the music scene that was the child of their collaboration and actually featured James Jagger (Mick's son) in a leading role as a musician leading a punk band - The Nasty Bits. This leads neatly into a section about Jagger and the cinema. The series that cost $100 million, portrays the New York music scene in the 1970s, and is awash in sex and drugs, but rock 'n' roll is giving way to an era of punk, disco and hip-hop.

Another celebrated film maker, Wes Anderson, has made use of several Stones tracks in his movies. In *THE ROYAL TENENBAUMS* he uses *Ruby Tuesday* when the main two protagonists finally get it together.

He uses the lesser-known song *2000 Man* during his directorial debut *BOTTLE ROCKET* where an attempted heist dissolves into a farce when everything goes wildly wrong.

The early song *I am Waiting* is featured in the comedic movie *RUSHMORE* where the lofty ambitions of the main character are given up as he follows in his father's footsteps.

Anderson employs the song *"Play With Fire"* when three brothers visit the mother who had abandoned them in *THE DARJEELING LMITED*

Finally, in his animated version of Roald Dahl's *FANTASTIC MR FOX,* The Rolling Stones' *"Street Fighting Man"* plays as three characters start to destroy the foxes' home.

Some other worthy mentions include the much more recent track *Doom and Gloom* in the Marvel Comics' " high grossing movie *"VENGERS: ENDGAME* from The Rousseau Brothers while a rocket ship is being fixed.

APOCAYPSE NOW has a great soundtrack but still finds room for *(I Can't Get No) Satisfaction* for a scene where Lance surfs behind a boat.

Benoit Blanc's *KNIVES OUT* features the track *Sweet Virginia* as Marta takes over the house and pours scorn on the people below her balcony.

Jagger and Film

I am certain that Jagger would have loved to have been accepted as a film star as well as a music icon but things have not really worked out as planned. I certainly admire his work as a producer on films like *Enigma* and there are one or two roles where he has shown that there is potential. I think that he carries such a strong persona with his music that it is difficult to see him in another light. One is always making the comparison whether consciously or not.

There is little doubt in my mind that his best performance is in the film that carries this same name –*Performance*. The Beatles had found success with their comedic
cinematographic roles so I am sure that the producers of
Performance hoped that Jagger, playing the role of a rock
star, would bring success to this movie. It is a very dark
and seedy portrayal of Swinging London full of sex and
drug references. I actually liked this seediness though it
does seem very dated today. Jagger, who scarcely speaks
in the first part of the film, performs the song *Memo From
Turner* with great menace and resolution.

There was a story that the sex in the movie was not
simulated but real. Rather like the Julie Christie / Donald
Sutherland scene in *Don't Look Now* that many claimed
was real sex, the titillating nature of this certainly got the
film talked about. My abiding memory from this film is
this scene with the two women in the bath – one of whom
is no other than Anita Pallenburg. She had been Brian
Jones's girlfriend until Keith won her away from him (as
I referenced, briefly, in the liaisons section) apparently
after he witnessed Jones assaulting her. She was Richards
partner till 1980. Richards believed as evidenced in his
best selling memoir *Life* that Anita and Jagger had a brief
liaison during the making of the film. It was denied but
certainly fitted the image of the band's "sex and drugs
and rock 'n' roll" supposed lifestyle.

Jagger's title role in the often-derided *Ned Kelly* (that
Irish accent notwithstanding) is perhaps a little unfair in
that even though he was probably a bit miscast, his acting
is not bad. We have to wait till the 2002 vehicle *The Man
From The Elysian Fields* where he gets a good part to

play and actually gets better reviews than Andy Garcia for his performance.

He has, of course, played the part of Michael Philip Jagger best of all in a number of documentaries and in all of the concert movies. He does appear a touch stilted in the Rock 'n ' Roll Circus movie that remained unreleased for a number of years. He is much more comfortable just playing himself in the Scorsese directed *Shine A Light*, the biographical *Being Mick* or the *Gimme Shelter* movie about Altamont. For someone who has appeared in front of so many cameras and recording devices he really ought to be used to it by now.

My understanding that the film *The Burnt Orange Heresy* is to be his last one. It premiered at the Venice Film Festival in 2019, Jagger playing Joseph Cassidy, an art dealer who forces a young couple into attempting to steal a painting from reclusive artist Jerome Debney, played by Donald Sutherland. It's a Faustian tale and Mick plays the devil who makes the deal with the art critic leading actor Claes Bang, who plays corrupt art critic James Figueras. Jagger and The Devil – now where have I heard that before? Giuseppe Capotondi stated that Jagger had added a "very elegant and sophisticated" element to his role, which he felt "was needed," but added that he hadn't discussed the possibility of the singer contributing to the movie soundtrack. This information comes courtesy of the online Ultimate Classic Rock from Martin Kielty on 15th September 2019.

I haven't seen the movie yet but it does appear that this might well be worth watching. Donald Sutherland has always been good value.

Tribute Bands

I remember seeing, on VH-1 many years ago, a programme from Wembley Stadium where The Stones were not going to be playing having cancelled for tax reasons and a tribute band accurately called The Counterfeit Stones did the programme instead with interviews as well as music. I recall Carlo Little, a very short lived drummer with The Rolling Stones, reminiscing how he rejected the group because he didn't think he would make any money. He worked as a session drummer in the 60's and ran a burger van outside Wembley. Now this certainly has more than a touch of irony.

The tribute band were actually reasonably good. It made me wonder just how many tribute bands there were out there and a cursory search reveals the following list in no particular order:

ST●NES MISCELLANY #10

The Counterfeit Stones
The Rolling Stones Now
Mick Jogger and the Rolling Zones
Not The Rolling Stones
Rollin Clones
Tumblin' Dice
Rolling Stoned
Let's Spend
The Night Together
Stikky Fingers
Sticky Fingers
Music City Stones
The Stones
Blushing Brides
HotRocks

Sixties
Mania
The Stoneleighs
Orange County Rolling Stones Tribute Band
Mick Adams & The Stones.
Chick Jagger & The Falling Rocks.
The Hollywood Stones
Jumping Jack Flash
Stony Rollers
Beggars Banquet
Stoned Acoustic
Roll The Stones
The Rolling Tones
Streetfighter
The US Stones
Satisfaction - The International Rolling Stones Show
The Rolling Stones Experience

There are a great many more in the USA that have the name of the respective city or state that they hail from, for example: Rolling Stones Cover Band Florida. With such a wealth of tribute bands who have chosen the music of the actual Stones with which to make a living, this can only be seen as a massive endorsement for the real thing. There are many imitators working professionally in the mainstream, too, who have been influenced by what is still called the greatest rock and roll band in the world.

I don't want to go into great depth here but suffice it to say that the following acts owe a great deal to The Stones. They provided a template by which all the bands which followed could use if they wanted too. Many did. Steve Tyler from Aerosmith owes much to The Stones as does David Johansen of New York Dolls and Primal Scream's Bobby Gillespie. The late Michael Hutchence, of the Australian band INXS, also had Jaggeresque tendencies. The newly reformed Black Crowes, who have supported the Stones on tour, are noted for churning out sensual blues-rock that recalls The Rolling Stones. Sheryl Crow, who has supported Jagger and the boys a few times, also owes them a debt for influencing some of her work as does Jon Bon Jovi.

Jerry Cantrell (Smashing Pumpkins) on a BBC radio show mentioned Steven Tyler and David Lee Roth as Jagger disciples. According to him, there wouldn't be any epic singer without Mick Jagger. He also added Mick Jagger is the forerunner of rock and roll. "It's amazing, the longevity, the attitude, just his ability to connect with the audience, to work a room. He is the archetype and the forerunner for what fronting a rock and roll band is all about."

The Black Crowes also have strong links with The Rolling Stones. (See the 1995 Wembley Concert review page 108). They have featured *Midnight Rambler, Can't You Hear Me Knocking* and *The Last Time* in their concert repertoire. Perhaps in keeping with the fact that the Stones have had problems with a few of their album covers, the Crowes' "Amorica" album, with a strand of a woman's pubic hair showing through bikini briefs, was banned in many places and a new cover without the hair or plain black cover was introduced.

Other notable disciples include Iggy Pop, Lenny Kravitz with whom Jagger has written songs, as has Dave Stewart, who co-wrote the *Alfie* 2004 version movie soundtrack which won the 2005 Golden Globes Award for *Old Habits Die Hard* and, recently, Jack White from the now defunct duo, The White Stripes. Even the great musical innovator, David Bowie is reported to have said that he wished he could be like Mick Jagger.

Steve Van Zandt, of E Street Band and *The Sopranos* fame, and a noted big Rolling Stones fan, writing in a *Rolling Stone Magazine* tribute to the band, commented on the acceptance of Jagger's voice especially on radio and claimed he broke open the door for everyone else. "Suddenly Eric Burdon and Van Morrison weren't so weird – even Bob Dylan". Van Zandt's "boss" from the E-Street band, Bruce Springsteen, was so influenced by the Stones that he used the second album to learn Keith's playing while still a teenager.

One dreads to think of the day when The Stones are no more, but their legacy will surely continue to live on through their music and concert films. Just as they, themselves, were influenced by Muddy Waters, Chuck Berry, Little Walter, Jimmy Reed and other blues legends, their influence will undoubtedly be felt by future bands.

Oasis, never far from controversy themselves, and perhaps more commonly linked with The Beatles, have recorded The Stones tracks *Street Fighting Man* with Liam Gallagher's Beady Eye group performing a very solid *Gimme Shelter*. They certainly had the swagger and attitude that that you used to get with the early Stones, too. Beady Eye have even recorded a song called *Beatles and Stones* extolling the virtues of both groups.

Chris Rea's *Stainsby Girls* who "love The Rolling Stones" has a great guitar riff (pure *Honky Tonk Women)* in the song, borrowed from Keith directly, but it is clearly a homage and not a rip off. This influence can also be traced through Keith Richard wannabees. Johnny

Thunders, again of the New York Dolls, Mick Jones of The Clash and Slash from Guns N' Roses are strong Richards impersonators. I know that Johnny Marr has a strong affinity to Keith, too, though his style is obviously different.

Mick and Keith, then, have a solid core of front line disciples as well as many others in lesser bands. Long may this continue.

London Olympic Games

After I heard that the organising Committee for the London Olympics were planning a best of British culture scenario for the opening ceremony. I wrote a letter reproduced below:

Katerinas, Stoupa,
Kalamata 24024
Messinia
Greece
28 September 2009

Sebastian Coe
Committee for the Planning of the
London Olympics

Dear Sebastian,

Please excuse the familiarity but having heard that you are looking to embrace the best of British culture in the Opening Ceremony for the Olympic Games in London, I felt that I had to write with a suggestion.

I live in the country where the Olympic Games originated and love most sport. I have another passion that I thought would help to represent the best of British culture. The Rolling Stones, who have been flying the flag for Britain since the early 1960s, would be an ideal advertisement for the games. They are one of the world's most iconic groups in the history of music.

We know that Mick Jagger loves his cricket and football. The Stones have performed at one of the world's biggest sporting events already. In 2006 they performed the halftime show at Superbowl XL to great acclaim and I know that if they could be persuaded to perform at the Olympics in their home town, London, then this would be a similar outstanding performance.

I do hope that you can at least consider this plea. I am sure it would be something to remember.

Yours sincerely,

Mike Heath

Mike Heath

eption +44 (0) 203 2012 000
+44 (0) 203 2012 001
w.london2012.com

Mr Mike Heath
Stoupa 24024
Messinias
Greece

14ᵗʰ October 2009

Dear Mike,

Thank you for your letter.

I was interested to hear your suggestion to involve the Rolling Stones in the London 2012 Olympic and Paralympic Games and I appreciate you taking the time to write to me personally.

I have passed your letter on to our Ceremonies Team for their interest. The many comments, thoughts and ideas that we have received so far bodes well for a healthy discussion over the next few years when planning for the London 2012 Ceremonies and Cultural Olympiad.

Thank you, once again, for writing – I appreciate your interest and support.

With best wishes,

Sebastian Coe KBE
Chairman

I was more than surprised to receive a prompt response from Seb Coe as you can see from the letter above.

As I mentioned, I had heard that the theme for the opening ceremony to the London games was going to be a celebration of "The Isles of Wonder", which would represent the whole of the country. Each succeeding opening ceremony at the Olympics has seemed to attempt to outdo the previous one. It is a game in itself. Glorifying what the country had to offer including a very rich musical heritage made me think of The Rolling Stones straight away. Their global image is second to none. Wouldn't be great, therefore, if they could appear in the opening ceremony with the whole world watching?

I could see reasons why The Stones might decline. The Palladium carousel incident and their later refusal to join in James Cordon's Carpool Karaoke on American TV, makes me think that they were never going to take part even if invited. They had, however, performed at the highly coveted Super Bowl halftime slot in 2006 so I held my breath. Lord Coe had written back personally to me, which I had not really expected, but I was still sceptical.

The closest we eventually got to The Stones making a contribution was a bit of their classic song *Satisfaction* being played along with many other British songs in a major medley. Hardly a real tribute to my heroes. That is not to say that British pop music should not have been celebrated. From time to time it has ruled the world. The Rolling Stones, as unofficial ambassadors, have led the way and continue on a global scale.

Unofficial Archive

Almost from the outset I have been collecting Rolling Stones "stuff". I have a huge collection of articles from newspapers, music papers and magazines that have interviews and features about the group. I have them filed away in my own archive. I also have a healthy collection of books by and about the group collectively and alone (see page 159).

I have friends who look out for Rolling Stones items in the press and receive daily Google Alerts relating to the group. A classic example is when Jagger appeared on the *Larry King Show* in the USA in May 2010 and, similarly on *Saturday Night Live*, I have a friend, George Shattuck, who organises recordings for me from American TV and sends them from Boston, Massachusetts for me to watch. I then turn them into DVDs.

I also have made (and continue to do so) over fifty double DVD sets which show all aspects of the group. This manifests itself in documentaries, concert footage, interviews, official pronouncements from the group themselves, news items, adverts etc. (See Appendix D for a detailed run down – page 223)

There are pictures below of the books and DVDs mentioned. I also have a vast collection of bootleg CDs from The Rolling Stones. The group have recently started to release their official bootlegs which I have, of course, purchased. One of the very best, and highly regarded, concert recordings of the group is the B*russels Affair* double CD from October 1973 from which I have a couple of versions as well as the official one that The Stones released in 2011. I would struggle to better the following verdict by John Harris, a British journalist, writer and critic when he wrote enthusiastically in The Guardian about this recording that it is "unimpeachably great: a beautifully recorded, often unhinged 70 minutes during which the Stones manage to sound like the Platonic ideal of a rock band: simultaneously tight, unhinged, absolutely convincing, and gloriously ludicrous". Some of my books and magazines pictured below:

Some of the bootleg CDs I have made of mainly the group but
some individual group members offerings too.

Some of the unofficial bootleg CDs including in the third row down, first on the left, the highly rated, and aforementioned, double *Brussels Affair* concert CD from 1973.

The DVD sets and below Volumes 52 and 53

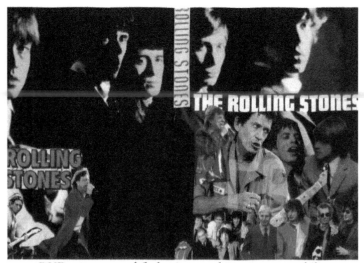

DVD set cover and (below) general Stones memorabilia

The following few pages show the subject matter of the DVDs that I have made. The first four or five are single disc sets but the rest are double disc sets making a hundred in total to date. Many of the items put onto disc are concert pieces either in full or stand out tracks. There are very many documentaries about the group or individual members past and present, too. The national news occasionally has a featured story which will, of course, get used. Things like The Stones songs used in TV advertising is covered in depth. You will probably be amazed at just how many there are. One set of recordings that show up on a number of the discs is the cover version of Stones songs by other artists. Many are excellent showing that the raw material with which they are working is very well written in the first place. I have recorded a number of things from foreign TV too.

I know that Bill Wyman, for example, became the group's archivist and I am certain that my efforts pale in comparison, but I do have a solidly comprehensive amount here. Something that is far too big to catalogue here, is the amount of articles from newspapers and magazines that I have collected. I, sadly, have very little from the very early days and the bulk of what I do have, covers the past twenty years in some great depth. The many articles from magazines, do, for example, tend to focus on all eras which helps to give a better overall picture especially of the early years during the sixties.

I have two or three people looking out for articles for me and they post them off to me. My sister, Barbara, is chief among these Stones spotters. These newspaper clippings and magazine articles currently fill half a dozen big folders under the sixteen headings below. They are not detailed here at all due to their size. They range from a single page to seven or eight pages or more and are mainly from Q, Mojo, Uncut, Classic Rock magazines and a range of tabloid and broadsheet newspapers, weekend supplements and fashion magazines.

The Google Alerts that I receive daily via the net are invariably a great help. If there is something about to happen I receive the notification and can act upon it when and wherever necessary.

1 Rolling Stones 1971-83
2 Rolling Stones 2000-07
3 Rolling Stones 2006
4 Rolling Stones 2008-09
5 Rolling Stones 2010
6 Rolling Stones 2011
7 Rolling Stones 2012
8 Rolling Stones 2013
9 Rolling Stones 2014
10 Rolling Stones 2015

11 Rolling Stones 2016
12 Rolling Stones 2017
13 Rolling Stones 2018
14 Rolling Stones 2019
15 Rolling Stones 2020 21
16 Rolling Stones 2022

Some of my general Rolling Stones memorabilia

I have an array of memorabilia from mugs, key rings, cuff links, a scarf. A shopping bag, a clock made from a Stones like vinyl LP, a tray with the famous tongue logo that my wife very kindly, and secretly, made for me at a local ceramics day class, a seat cushion from the 2003 concert at Twickenham. These are displayed above.

I have always liked the game Monopoly and having had versions from the USA, another with Athens, Greece landmarks as well as the London based one. Imagine my joy when I was able to purchase a Rolling Stones version. This joy failed to persist for long, however, as none of my family or friends would play, assuming that I had some sort of advantage being such an avid fan. The game remains in its virgin state something that is not always easy to associate with the Rolling Stones. I have never played it…yet.

Below is a framed picture showing the various infamous tongue motifs "through the ages". The final one dating from the *Blue and Lonesome* era.

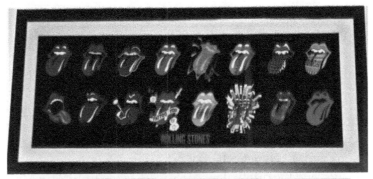

Official Stones DVDs plus the Monopoly set. (Below) My Gered Mankowitz "Red Cage" print Number 45/200 from 1999.

The item I prize above all others for very obvious reasons is my Gered Mankowitz print. It is called "Red Cage" and the original pictures were taken in 1965 in Mason's Yard, London. I have had it framed and it now hangs in our bedroom. It is hand signed in pencil and numbered 45 out of just 200 prints. Sandra was not that keen to have it above the mantle piece in our living room and it was sadly consigned to the landing stairway where it was it was partnered with a twenty fifth wedding anniversary present, a painting of John Lee Hooker and rarely seen by friends and neighbours.

A year ago after decorating the landing and our bedroom, I did manage to have it moved into our bedroom. It is a very big room and the print does not overpower anything. Of course, it is now not seen by anyone apart from Sandra and me. It is, in fact, a great sight to greet you when you wake up in the morning. I paid about £200 for it twenty years ago when it was first issued but see that it can cost from between £650 and £850 from different London Galleries. You are invited to make bids for the print. There was one that was sold in 2015 where the auctioneer decided not to divulge the amount it sold for. I never bought it as an investment but as a work of art but it is certainly gratifying to see that its value has much increased.

A copy of Mankowitz's original photograph

Tee Shirts

Some of my Rolling Stones Tee Shirts. The motto on a couple read: "Some of us grew up listening to the

Rolling Stones. The cool ones still do" and "Never underestimate an old man who listens to The Rolling Stones. Below a 57th Anniversary Celebratory Tee Shirt.

My 70th Birthday

Some of the presents I received on my seventieth birthday. The most treasured and still untouched is the bottle of Jose Cuervo Tequila Rolling Stones edition. I use other non specialist bottles to make my Tequila sunrises and margarita drinks. I don't really want to open this bottle. Thank you, John and Mary Cole, – a very thoughtful and cherished present.

I did receive other non-Rolling Stones presents, as a friend said 'proper presents' but they have no place here.

5th June 2018 Old Trafford, Manchester No Filter Tour: (The latest concert I attended)

Having not seen The Stones live since the Twickenham gig in 2003, I was extremely keen to see this latest No Filter incarnation. Of course I had seen the triumph at Glastonbury on TV and had the Hyde Park Mark II and Havana, Cuba DVDs so I knew the quality was still there. Living in Greece since 2007 did present a problem – and they haven't played Athens in a long while – with the expense of air travel and ticket pricing. A family wedding in Cornwall came to the rescue: we would be in the UK at the time when the Stones were playing some of their UK shows.

My wife has never been a Rolling Stones fan, as I have already mentioned, despite my pleading but she had accompanied me to the Twickenham gig as shown earlier. The support act was Starsailor and she really liked them even though her daddy was not an alcoholic! I specifically mention her at this point because she worked damned hard to get me two tickets for the Manchester show when I had given up in despair. Phoning from Greece was not the easiest task. I saw that the support act for this show was Richard Ashcroft, late of The Verve and would have preferred Elbow who were supporting at other gigs. It had been rumoured that Liam Gallagher was going to be the support but once he found out the venue, and, as a diehard Man City fan, he was never going to perform at Old Trafford. Shame on him.

Richard Ashcroft was surprisingly good. I had seen him once or twice on TV live and he, like Ian Brown of The Stone Roses sometimes had issues with pitch and tuning. His set was strong as was his voice. The lead guitarist was similarly excellent. He played a number of the old Verve hits and I loved the irony that he finished with *Bitter Sweet Symphony*. This was the song that had sampled too greater a part of The Andrew Loog Oldham Orchestra's version of The Stones early classic *The Last Time*. The case culminated in royalties to Jagger and Richards and their names added as co-writers. I heard some time after the concert that Jagger and Richards had relented and yielded their names as co- writers which would greatly favour The Verve members as far as royalties were concerned. They really don't need the money.

I went with my brother Paul who had accompanied me to the 1969 Hyde Park concert but hadn't seen them since that time. A mere forty nine year gap! We arrived at Old Trafford to be met with very strict security which was not surprising since the bombing the previous year at the Ariana Grande concert at the Manchester Arena had left twenty three people dead. We took our seats just as Richard Ashcroft came on to be met by two uncomfortable issues. The very bright sun was directly in our eyes and did not disappear behind the Stretford End Stand until exactly 8.20pm just as The Stones were introduced. What a coincidence! Even with sunglasses the light was very intimidating. The second issue affected me, rather than Paul, in that I could not get my legs in a comfortable position because the seats in front were too close. I have never had this problem at Twickenham   (or Wembley Stadium for that matter). I think they have catered better for typical rugby supporters in a more favourable way. I bruised the bone just below my knee on my left leg and had to sit side saddle in order to gain some comfort. This meant twisting my neck to see the stage and screens. I still enjoyed the Ashcroft set.

As soon as The Stones were heralded by the MC everyone stood up almost as one which gratified me greatly. I didn't have carry on contorting myself into uncomfortable, unnatural positions any more.

Two and a quarter hours later as the gig climaxed with its now traditional pyrotechnic display, my feet ached a little but my head was swimming with, dare I say, satisfaction and joy.

Paul remarked that he was amazed just how good the concert had been. Apart from the performance of the band, which was similarly amazing, I was really taken with the demographic of the audience. The majority of the crowd were young - not screaming teenagers but people in their twenties and thirties. Thinking back audiences at other Stones concerts, I had been to over the years, were usually of an older demographic - predominantly the same age as me. Aged 72 at that time, and just three years younger than the main two protagonists, I had not expected to see this. I did find this cross generational aspect very encouraging. It might be part of the Glastonbury effect where they went down a storm but certainly testament to the lasting appeal of the group. Rock shows do have the capacity to unite generations, as can any good music, and I saw large numbers of parents with their (older) children all singing along to the familiar songs.

The show opened with a major classic *Jumpin' Jack Flash* and straightaway I was impressed with the strength of Jagger's voice. Apart from the song *Shattered* which I felt was a little rushed, I could not fault any song. Even old grizzy voiced Richards, with his usual allotment of two songs midway through, sounded cool -*You Got The Silver* in particular. Jagger's blues harp was soon put to use in the, sadly, only number from the very successful and recent *Blue and Lonesome* album with the song *Just Your Fool*. I had remarked to Paul that they would do *Ride 'em On Down* next, as I knew that they had included two numbers from that album quite often on this leg of the tour. They didn't, but followed with the audience request song *Let's Spend The Night Together*. It was here that he started his usual walk and skip to either side of the stage and then onto the walkway that led straight into the audience. He managed to unbutton his shirt while holding the mike and singing as he strutted his stuff with perhaps slightly less gusto than in 2003. The audience sang along to this (as with many of the set list) in splendid voice. All those people near me with their little phones filming the performance must have picked up the voices of their neighbours quite loudly singing out of tune which perhaps spoils the whole purpose of the recording. The desire to record everything especially for social media seems paramount. The old holding up of your cigarette lighter to certain songs is a thing of the past in this technological age.

This song was followed by a very strong version of *Like A Rolling Stone* by which time he had shed the shirt to reveal a black T-shirt. More strutting and a very cool harp solo midway through. I had forgotten just how good their version of the Dylan song is.

I was really impressed with Ronnie Wood's guitar playing, too, and it appeared to me that he has now taken on the mantle of the main guitarist. Keith, though obviously no slouch, likes to gesture, freeze frame certain manoeuvres with his arm or leg like a follow through with a golf shot. He does, however, still play a mean riff. The weaving that the two guitarists are celebrated for, where they often claim that they do not know who is playing which bit, seems to favour Ronnie more strongly. I am not suggesting that Keith is past it just that his contribution is perhaps a little less than it used to be. The overall sound is still very good and that, of course, is everything. Chuck Leavell's piano playing sparkled throughout and you have to marvel that The Stones have been blessed with such great pianists throughout their longevity. Chuck's playing is as good as any of his predecessors - Ian Stewart and Nicky Hopkins.

Sympathy For The Devil is always a land mark song and, at Old Trafford, Manchester, the four giant screens above the stage showed images of a fire raging out of control while the "woo woos" from the audience echoed around the stadium Jagger's vocal was again really strong as, indeed, the lyrics warrant.

Then, for me, the absolute stand out song of the night was *Miss You*. Jagger on guitar, a great driving beat from Charlie augmented by Daryl Jones's wonderfully funky base lines and excellent solo and a wild saxophone solo. Disco at its very best. Magnificent. I used to think that this was a good song but the current live version lifts it to "great" status. They may repeat old songs but they can still freshen them up.

Midnight Rambler allowed Ronnie free rein in a role that Mick Taylor used to excel in. I love the changing tempos in this song usually a great stomping song but the very slow section near the end permits Jagger to do his "Oh Yeahs" to the audience who reciprocate with gusto. Tonight they cleverly segued in the old Blues favourite *You Gotta Move* towards the end of the song. The lighting was an integral part of this song too. The four screens would all flash red on and off as Ronnie's guitar stridently played out the final speeded up section of the song. Highly dramatic. Their light shows are totally modern.

The show ended, as it usually does, with *Brown Sugar, Gimme Shelter* and *Satisfaction.* All favourites and ripe for encore performances. For many people *Gimme Shelter* is their top Stones song and over the years the female vocalist gets a chance to shine next to Jagger. Merry Clayton was the first on record and a performance which is hard to better. I had come to highly rate Lisa Fischer's version in recent times but she has now undertaken a deserved solo career and, in Manchester, this role was more than ably filled by Sasha Allen. A chance to shine which she most certainly did.

The atmosphere throughout was electric and the energy displayed by Jagger, in particular, fed into the excited audience. To me they have been better every time I have seen them and, at the risk of sounding petulant, those doubters perhaps ought to attend a concert before sneering about being them being too old. The shows are designed wonderfully with the lighting and visual effects and, as a testament to growing old disgracefully, the Rolling Stones are still in first place.

ST●NES MISCELLANY #11

Set List Manchester:
Jumpin' Jack Flash
It's Only Rock 'n' Roll (But I Like It)
Tumbling Dice
Shattered Just Your Fool
Let's Spend the Night Together
Like a Rolling Stone
You Can't Always Get What You Want
Paint It Black
Honky Tonk Women
You Got the Silver
Before They Make Me Run
Sympathy for The Devil
Miss You
Midnight Rambler (with a snippet of You Gotta Move)
Start Me Up
Brown Sugar
Gimme Shelter
(I Can't Get No) Satisfaction

Jagger is The Rolling Stones

The one thing that is obvious to me is that Mick Jagger is The Rolling Stones. You could argue a case for Keith, too, but guitarists have been changed/ replaced within the group and there has been minimal difference. Ronnie, to me has stepped up and has filled Mick Taylor's shoes very ably. They have had three excellent pianists. Even the late, brilliant, saxophonist Bobby Keys has been successfully replaced. Take Jagger out of the equation and replace him with someone else and it will be like the mishmash they have created with Queen when they had the wonderful Paul Rodgers fronting the group or Paul Lambert now. That is someone AND Queen. Replacing Jagger would be the same. It would be whoever and The Rolling Stones. The heart would have been taken out of the group. Keith and Ronnie have had the X-Pensive Winos and The New Barbarians in the past, so I am sure they could continue in some form. I think Keith, like the old bluesmen he admires, is destined to play until he drops. Of course his song writing partnership with Jagger is of ultra-importance. Keith is known as the riffmeister, a title I personally don't like very much, but there is absolutely no denying that his contribution to the music in the partnership is great indeed. They are not called the Glimmer Twins for nothing. I just think that now, in 2020/21, his role has started to be overtaken by Ronnie as far as the playing is concerned.

Jagger and Richards do have ten out of *Rolling Stone Magazine's* top 500 songs in the 2012 edition, matched only by Dylan and The Beatles, and this most certainly cannot, nor should not, be dismissed. It is amazing in itself – but others can, and have, performed great cover versions of those songs. I am saying, therefore, that it is the performance that Jagger has brought to The Stones, and to the world at large, that would be irreplaceable.

I repeat my opening line to this section – Mick Jagger is The Rolling Stones. Having said all of this there was something strange about the four BBC documentaries on the lives of the Rolling Stones from mid-2022. Mick, Keith, Ronnie and the late Charlie Watts were each given an hour-long documentary. Everything was well produced giving a detailed insight into their lives as Rolling Stones. The mechanics of the group was well detailed...or was it? Where was Bill Wyman and his 30-year contribution? Glyn Johns, the legendary record producer who has worked with the Beatles, Led Zep and the Who as well as the Stones, is reported as claiming the Wyman/Watts rhythm section as the greatest of all time. Higher praise would be difficult to find. So why has Wyman been virtually airbrushed from this version of the story. We see glimpses of him but no mention. This is not the place to try to guess why but the point needs to be made.

ROLLING STONES SONG ANAGRAMS

ANSWERS (from page 78)

Solve these TEN Rolling Stones' Classic Song Anagrams.

The number in brackets of each clue refers to the number of words in the answer.

1 PET RATS UM (3) START ME UP
2 IN A FAST OCTIS (1) SATISFACTION
3 FISH MUCK GANJA LPJ (3) JUMPING JACK FLASH
4 IT BACK IN LAP (3) PAINT IT BLACK
5 YON THOWN KNOKEM (3) HONKY TONK WOMEN
6 FOFOT CLYDE OF GUM (5) GET OFF OF MY CLOUD
7 WISH DROLES (2) WILD HORSES
8 WROB GANSUR (2) BROWN SUGAR
9 TROT IDOLER LESTER (3) LITTLE RED ROOSTER
10 RESIT VOWAL NOL (4) IT'S ALL OVER NOW

Lockdown

With most of the world in a surreal lockdown through 2020 and 2021peoples lives were forced to change. There were no theatres and certainly no music concerts. Resorting to Zoom people were able to communicate and there were some music collaborations.

The Stones did a slightly comic version of *You Can't Always Get What You Want* with Charlie playing non existent drums. Vocals and guitar work were excellent as were the invisible drums.

Their release of *Ghost Town,* which was a reworking of an existing song adapted to make the lyrics fit the pandemic, actually topped the iTunes downloads chart in 2020.

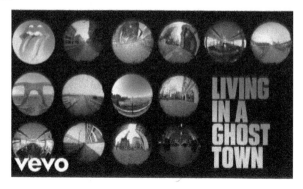

The following year, after even more noises about tracks for a new album, Jagger contacted an old friend in Dave Grohl of the Foo Fighters and together they put out a rip roaring, pub rock meets punk, track taking the mickey out of the lockdown and pandemic. *Eazy Sleazy* shows that, at 77 years of age, Jagger's writing skills have nor diminished.

The following pictures are screen grabs from the video.

This does make one hungry for this elusive new album which has been promised for years. Keith is certainly up for it, too. We might not have to wait too much longer after all.

APPENDIX A

POPULAR MUSIC PROJECT

Introduction from a previous TMA (U203 08) which underlined my topic and approach

For this project I am undertaking an examination of the Rolling Stones album "Beggars Banquet" (1968) and The Sex Pistols "Never Mind The Bollocks" (1976), taking into especial account their respective musical styles and structures, modes of production, social meanings and historical significance.

The two groups – the Stones (particularly in the late 1960s and early 70s) and the Pistols (over a much shorter self-destructive period in the late 70s) are, perhaps, the epitome of youth subcultural music. A detailed analysis, therefore, of their music, the thinking behind it and the ways in which it helped to shape (or lead?) certain youth groups ought to prove interesting. Too often, today, modern popular music is dismissed as trivial and meaningless. I hope to show mainly through sociological approaches that this is not necessarily true.

What are termed "oppositional forms of popular culture" or "cultures of resistance" need to be examined so that the much publicized generation gap and general breakdown of the family unit can be placed in context.

The issue of class will also be addressed, too, in order to determine where support for these groups was based – and why.

My primary objective is to examine the cultural implications rather than the music as just music although we must not forget that this latter is important too.

Despite the oft- heard criticism from some sections of society that they "cannot hear the words" on modern songs, I want to devote particular attention to the lyric content of both groups' songs. It has to be of crucial importance to determine the message. How important are the words? Is there really a social message? What is the role of the songs in what is termed the cultural and ideological struggles of their time? It will be necessary to relate the songs on these albums partly to other material by the same artists and, more importantly, to other contemporary styles.

A little later in my introduction (to TMA 08) I listed the songs on the two albums

Beggars Banquet The Rolling Stones: Sympathy For The Devil / No Expectations / Dear Doctor / Parachute Woman / Jigsaw Puzzle / Street Fighting Man / Prodigal Son / Stray Cat Blues / Factory Girl / Salt Of The Earth

Never Mind The Bollocks The Sex Pistols: Holidays In The Sun / Bodies / No Feelings / Liar / God Save The Queen / Problems / Seventeen / Anarchy In The UK / Submission / Pretty Vacant / New York / EMI

Assignment U203 09

"You had to put out a 45, a red hot single every three months. An album was something like Motown – you put the hit single on the album and ten tracks of shit and then rush it out. Now the album is the thing" Keith Richards in 1971.

"When we signed The Sex Pistols it was clear that their flame was going to burn brightly but briefly... It couldn't survive because as soon as they made their first LP that was the end because the whole idea of making an LP was counter-revolutionary. Albums are part of the then-generation and then they made an album." Al Clark (Virgin Records)

I aim to start by looking briefly at the historico-political scene at the time when both albums were issued. I will also give a general summary of the respective groups' musical style before a much more specific and detailed reference to the albums. The music of the time (1968 and 1976) will show the generally bland, sanitised type of record that topped the Pop charts. The subcultural aspect of The Rolling Stones and The Sex Pistols music will play a major part of this project in the form of what are called "oppositional cultures". Because The Rolling Stones are still very much with us, and, in a way, part of the Rock establishment at least, it is sometimes forgotten just how much they were seen as rebels, outcasts and generally subversive. Perhaps they paved the way for Punk?

Beggars Banquet appeared in 1968. This was the apocalyptic year which saw Martin Luther King and Bobby Kennedy assassinated; a 100,000 strong crowd march to the Pentagon to protest at U.S. involvement in the Viet Nam War; student revolution in universities in Europe and The USA – notably in Paris (where there appeared to be very legitimate grounds). In this country, student and political demonstrations were dealt with harshly, particularly as exemplified by the provocative behaviour of the police at the anti-Viet Nam Grosvenor Square "demo". Mick Jagger, of the Rolling Stones, was

185

in the student ranks and among those charged by the police.

"The time is ripe for fighting in the street" (Street Fighting Man) – revolution was perhaps in the air. Bennett (in Unit 18) refers to the collapse of hegemony between 1966 -70. The period, he noted "witnessed the development of a 'control culture' exercised, principally, against the student left and the permissive counterculture".

Authoritarianism and working class resistance under the Law and Order Society was prevailing when punk reared its head in 1976. Compared with the 1960s, the '70s witnessed an apparently intractable economic situation. There was mass youth unemployment, high inflation, and for that section of society which suffered most – working class school leavers (particularly those without qualifications) – there really was in Johnny Rotten's words "No Future" With a complete rejection of their past, punks sought, as the blank generation, a "nowhere" to inhabit. I will be exploring the anarchic and nihilistic nature of the lyrics later.

Suffice it to say, at this point, that perhaps the most striking innovation of Punk was the introduction of political subject matter into Rock music.

The Stones started in a world where suits and ties were still the order of the day. Their unkempt appearance continually got them ejected from restaurants and hotels for example. Their music was built on raw R & B. They appeared arrogant, aggressive, outrageous and ever contemptuous of that Establishment which sought to destroy them. They were supported by those teenagers who realised that the Stones were "kicking hard against solid, staid conventions in order to live life the way they feel it". Their post-war urban blues music was now being shouted into the big white world. Carr, in predictably journalistic style (but nonetheless accurately) notes "with swashbuckling insolence they kissed off the staid mainstream of popular music by going 180 degrees against existing trends, channelling their natural primal brashness into.....their songs and using it to mirror the frustrations and boredom of the time".

I aim to devote most of the available space to "Street Fighting Man" and "Sympathy For The Devil" though I will refer to the songs on "Beggars Banquet". The style and structure of songs on "Banquet" is varied. Technically their best album to date, the Stones still present a number of traditional blues songs with typical three line lyric (AAB) set to a 12 bar chord and sometimes a four line lyric (ABAB). As Keith Richards (lead guitar) himself has stated "looking back at '20s and '30s blues records, I realised that many were in strange tunings. I started to use open tunings on "Beggars Banquet". I eventually got into open-D tuning – D A D F# A D (low to high)". He uses acoustic guitar sometimes with a slide and bottleneck playing on the blues tracks ("Prodigal Son", "No Expectations", "Dear Doctor" and "Parachute Woman"). "Stray Cat Blues" which Jagger admits to stealing the feel, pace and whole sound from Lou reed's song "Heroin", is a much more Rock orientated song with Jimi Hendrix free form style guitar playing. The lyrics, however, about underage sex, fit the blues pattern. "Factory Girl" has a country/folk feel to it vocally and instrumentally. "Salt Of The Earth" and especially "Jigsaw Puzzle" with their ABAB lyric patterns and choruses contain a lot of Dylanesque references. Before returning to "Street Fighting Man" and "Sympathy", a general word about structure and style from "Never Mind The Bollocks" by the Sex Pistols. While the Stones' album contains some form of variety, the Pistols' LP is, to borrow Phil Spector's phrase, a "wall of sound". This sound is a barrage of guitars with treble turned to maximum relentlessly pursuing unmelodic lines against a background of turbulent cacophonic drumming and screamed vocals. Lewis claims what made the Pistols survive was the fact that "they were able to put a sound to their behaviour i.e. their music. It came at a time when young people… were fed up with poppy-type music." Punk supplied a new rhythm and vitality.

When looking at "God Save The Queen "and "Anarchy In The UK" in greater detail, I will explore their innovatory vocal style. Instrumentally, as Frith notes, punk was constricted by its realist claims "by its use of melodic structures and a rhythmic base that were taken to tell-it-like-it-was, just because they followed rock 'n' roll rules – the 4:4 beat, shouted vocals, rough guitar, bass, drums line up". There was little innovation here. "Paranoid" by Black Sabbath (1970) is a typically heavy metal version of Rock. There are close links between the two styles as can be heard. The "Never Mind" album is literally an assault upon the ear of the listener. From the marching feet that take us into "Holidays In The Sun" up to its final track with its angry response to A & M Records tucked on to the end of EMI, the album is structured into an almost non-stop attack on the established form of mainstream Rock and Pop, and on society through its anarchic, subversive("God Save The Queen", "Holidays In The Sun"), nihilistic ("Pretty Vacant", "Problems", "17",

"Submission") and generally offensive lyrics ("Bodies", "EMI", "New York"). The overriding impression is that of repetition. As pointed out in Unit 16, the wholesale repetition generates a feeling of tight solidarity and almost "given the timbre, vocal attack, noise level and use of accent – one of mob violence". In the Pistols' songs, this repetition of complete phrases suggests a deliberate attempt to be provocatively quasi-mindlessly banal – the blank generation. It is difficult to accept the Pistols' songs as songs (as opposed to statements) but they do generally follow the same pattern – the 4:4 beat from Rock 'n' Roll as mentioned above. Each song is predictable rhythmically in that a regular beat is totally predominant. The drumming and cymbals are heard on almost every beat. There is little differentiation of fore and backgrounds texturally – the music is heard as a whole. The AAB pattern is predominant musically and the lyrics follow different rhyme schemes for the verses (ABAB, AABB even ABCC) with only the chorus used for an almost collage approach of shouted statements – it is here that vocal and backing can be heard in opposition to one another or the backing yielding to allow space for the vocal comment.

Probably because I have made little reference to "Street Fighting Man" and "Sympathy For The Devil" yet, the impression given of "Beggars Banquet" is that it is a blues album. It is difficult to deny the blues feel but these two tracks – the two most notorious ones – have their base in Rock. The aggression and violence though more subtle (and sophisticated?) than the Sex Pistols' output is, nonetheless, present and viewed in the context of "sleepy London Town" ("Street Fighting Man") in

189

1968, it created quite a reaction – perhaps an overreaction – in establishment quarters.

Ev 'ry where I hear the sound of march – ing, charg – ing feet, boy

'cause Sum – mers here and the time is right for fight – ing in the street, boy

"Street Fighting man" opens with a basic, compulsive drum rhythm emphasised by both rhythm guitar and bass, magnifying the impact of the on beat. Together they provide a dynamic thrust forward and it is against this that Jagger has to sing – in fact, fight to sing. It is a simple opposition but exactly right. The way the words are emphasised is important. The accent falls relentlessly. The revolution is on the march – charging through the music. The radical protest movement adopted the song as an anthem yet theirs is hardly the cause the words underwrite:

Where I live the game to play is compromise solution These words fit more accurately the Western world's "sleepy" political climate. This perhaps tells us that the politics of the Rolling Stones were more symbolic than literal. The words are evasive but as Dalton tells us "the Stones' politics have always been the politics of delinquency in the tradition of Eddie Cochran's 'Summertime Blues'. They have no need to indulge in justifying lyrics". Jagger himself has often played this to the full as in "Sympathy For The Devil", for instance, with:

What's puzzling you is the nature of my game. Perhaps a very suitable epithet? Jagger decides that:

There's just no place for Street Fighting Man so

What can a poor boy do 'cept sing for a rock 'n' roll band?

Keith Richards tells us that the song was recorded on a mono cassette "with very distorted over recording". The sitar – an instrument used in hippie music – plays long open notes in the turmoil of the background. The music is very aggressive – perhaps more so than the lyric –from the beginning to the powerful climax. The way in which notes and words pile up against each other at the end of each verse has been likened to a crowd rushing a police barrier. It is not hard to hear this if you want to. The long open notes combined with the repeated menacing descent of the bass line, marching alongside it. This rhythm, notes Landau, first used by the Beatles on "Walrus" is based on the oscillations of English police sirens.

"The melody is insignificant but the sound is sensational" raved the Melody Maker over an earlier Rolling Stones song. It is this all over sound that is important. Just as the aggressive and cruder Sex Pistols' sound threatened violence, then the strident chords of "Street Fighting Man" also implied menace. Dalton commented that the violence of the Stones "has always been a surrogate for the larger violence their audience is so obviously capable of". Jagger, himself, has often stated that violence in Rock could never be harnessed for social change because it is undirected. When asked by "Der Spiegel" if "Street Fighting Man" was subversive, he replied "Yes, of course, but don't ever expect a record to start a revolution". Keith Richards has echoed his same point when claiming that people attend Stones' concerts "to work out" (Surrogate violence?). "Teenagers are not screaming over music anymore but for deeper reasons. We are just giving them an outlet." The Stones have always made it clear that they are anti-establishment in general. Contemporary society is often a target – one thing is clear today, they have been sufficiently cynical to learn how to manipulate it to their own ends. Perhaps this is the real message. The Satanist, Kenneth Anger once said that the Stones "are too anarchic to ever really be a menace".

This interesting comment could be applied to the Sex Pistols as well.

I am the antichrist I am an anarchist

I don't know what I want but I know how to get it

I wanna destroy the passer-by

'cos I

I wanna be anarchy   No dogsbody......

And I wanna be anarchy... Know what I mean

'cos I wanna be an anarchist

Get pissed...destroy

Words from the banned and withdrawn track "Anarchy in the UK", which if taken literally, posed a real threat to society. Before discussing the song, one has to bear in mind Johnny Rotten's words from a 1980 interview: "I think you've got to be an idiot to think that any of that meant anything. It changes nothing....It's escapism. All music is". (Echoes here of Jagger and his "what can a poor boy do 'cept sing in a rock 'n' roll band". Unit 19 refers to the "cosmetic rage" of anarchism. How far was the music of the Pistols a press stunt or a genuine reflection of political concern? We may never know. Just as "Street Fighting Man" and "Sympathy" are open to a number of interpretations, and probably deliberately so, then the Pistols' music is too. The overwhelming tone of "Anarchy" is violence, unbridled aggression, destruction. From the demonic laugh through to the sudden screaming, screeching end, the guitars, drums and sneering vocal conspire to hurl their attack our way. The words are clear – which is often not the case in Pistols' records – they are meant to be heard. The words are clearly enunciated.

Destroy ya! The voice is proletarian. Is the message for the masses? A clue to it not being such a positive statement comes in the lines:

Anarchy in the UK

It's coming sometime... maybe

This may have been deliberately vague, too. Certainly the feeling of hopelessness is evident. It also shows the limitations of putting political thought into music.

Rotten's singing style rejects both the rather colourless clarity of Progressive Rock and the "white soul" modes (adopted by Jagger among others), replacing it with an apparently artless, natural vocal approach with roots in the cockney novelty singing of Anthony Newley and David Bowie as well as the chanting of football fans. Frith deems this style as the most significant innovation of Punk Rock at the level of musical sound "since its effect is to represent within a communications medium a form of expression which was previously merely the object of media reproach" A working class voice was possible beyond the comic novelty of character actors. Laing cites Rotten as developing "an explicitly working class voice by using proletarian accents, expressing an inarticulateness". Hebdige (from Radio 8) echoes this in talking of a "flat, unemotional, alien voice in one dimension and positively demonic at times in Pistols' songs".

"God Save The Queen", probably the most notorious and important Pistols' song – if only through massive media coverage – taken in conjunction with "Anarchy" appear in Hebdige's view as a "symbolic act of treason". Punks capitulated to alienation. Whereas black urban youth, through Reggae, could place themselves in an imagined elsewhere (Africa, The West Indies) punks were tied to present time. They were bound to a Britain with "No Future"

God save the Queen   A fascist regime

Made you a moron   A potential H-bomb

God save the Queen   She ain't no human being

There ain't no future in England's dreaming

Just as Punk concerts spitting on the audience became the "accepted" thing, then the words in "God Save the Queen" are spat out. The one dimensional voice is clearly to be heard here. Just as Jagger's so-called pact with Lucifer on "Sympathy For The Devil" has become legend, we can almost hear the positively maniacal, demonic voice of Rotten, sounding as if he is possessed by "outside" forces.. The typical driving guitar and drums with cymbals heard on every beat, serve to emphasise these alien forces. In a harsh, staccato, style, the song expresses a cynical and critical view of the monarchy. The words reproduced above are deliberately overstated in a calculated way to cause maximum outrage. The succinct irony of the lyric is found in lines like:

God save the Queen 'cos tourists are our money

Our figurehead is not what she seems

The dry, stuttering machine gun instrumentation overtakes the vocal at times. We get an abstract overall noise. Radio 8 notes that the best lines are almost thrown away:

We're the poison in the machine

There is heavy sarcasm in: *We mean it maam*

Political threat coupled with biological reality in:

We're the future   Your future

The song ends on the repeated line:

No future in England's dreaming   No future...

perhaps an accurate diagnosis of the surfeit of regressive nostalgia involved in the then current Silver Jubilee celebrations. To release the record at such a time caused the (intended) maximum shock and distaste and helped the Pistols live up to their folk-devil image. The choice of the same title as the National Anthem was an especially effective blow against ruling class propaganda. The Pistols could have used the same tune but chose an oppositional "melody" for their purpose. When Laurie Hall (EMI Records) was asked if he saw the Pistols as a cultural threat, he dismissed the notion claiming "I don't think they pose any threat.... they represent the voice of the kids on the streets...they created their own music which was very raw and very violent on occasions".

Derek Green (A & M Records) similarly regards the attack on society as "naïve and innocent...not well thought out" while defending their right as individuals to "knock" the establishment. (Certainly this was true but most of their followers would have been politically naïve as well). The type of record buyer would therefore not have to be a revolutionary to buy Sex Pistols' records any more than those buying Rolling Stones' records. We return to the music as surrogate rebellion argument. F & J Vermorel note the links with Situationist Internationale (see below) that were employed by the Pistols along with Marxist leanings. It is not difficult to make such links. Burchill & Parsons take a different stance – more in keeping with "The Great Rock 'n' Roll Swindle" film as put out by the Pistols at a later date (minus it has to be said Johnny Rotten). The press stunt and use of social disorder as a marketing technique theory is propounded. The commercialisation of Punk that was clearly seen by Malcolm MacLaren (the Pistols' puppet master) does not concern us here but should not be forgotten.

Frith's Keighley survey highlights the importance of music for pupils who rejected their class cultures whether middle-class rejecting success or working-class rejecting work. Songs like "Problems", "Pretty Vacant", "17", reflect this rejection of the work ethic. The "Daily Mirror" quotation (from Vermorel) provides the justification for Punk: "In a single month 104,000 school leavers have gone... to an idle purposeless life on the dole... is it any wonder they turn to anarchistic heroes like Johnny Rotten?"

You're only 29   got a lot to learn

But when your money dies   you will not return....

See my face, not a trace, no reality

I don't work, I just speed   that's all I need

I'm a lazy sod   I'm a lazy sod....... (from "17")

Situationist Internationale (founded 1957) had its ideas put into current use by the Sex Pistols. For example, the concept of 'detournement' which is turning the establishment's codes and values (i.e. the Hit Parade) against itself, or the notion of 'recuperation' whereby the establishment (i.e. record companies) absorbs criticism by patronising it turning its negative (i.e. creative) value into positive (i.e. celebratory and appreciated) values.

Whether the motives of the Sex Pistols can be questioned, one cannot deny that largesections of disillusioned working-class youth did identify with them. Sophie's diary (again from Vermorel) makes a solid point: "The Pistols like the Rolling Stones are feeding rebellious stances, making the kids question to a degree."

The Stones' attitude to politics has always been more anarchistic than socialist "manifesting an indifference to specific events, while offsetting it with massive assaults on all forms of bourgeois quackery" (Dalton). Their revolution has never concerned itself with details. By "Beggars Banquet", Jagger was able to cast himself in the role that parents had given him – evil incarnate. He became, on stage, a cynical, scoffing, fiendish figure who had power over his audience. Consequently there came "Sympathy For The Devil" – a black Saturnine number in which Lucifer – King of Darkness – is protagonist, dancing attendance at the world's disasters:

I was around when Jesus Christ had his moment of doubt and faith

I made damn sure that Pilate washed his hands and sealed his fate.....

I stuck around St Petersburg when I saw it was time for a change....

I rode a tank, held a gen'ral's rank when the Blitzkrieg raged and the bodies stank...

I shouted 'who killed the Kennedys?....

In this highly literate song, full of imagery and incident – known and understood by his audience –many people have, perhaps, naively interpreted a Satanic pact between the powers of darkness and the Stones. Especially in the aftermath of the murders at Altamont, while this song was being performed, this complicity with evil has been cited as proof. Schofield, after noting that a "whiff of Satanism" was useful for pepping up the image of the Rolling Stones, declares; "Mick himself never had more than a dilettante's involvement with the powers of darkness – it was just one of his games to pretend he was". "Sympathy", based on Bulgakov's novel "The Master and Margarita", like the novel highlights one corrupt establishment being overthrown only to become corrupt. This forms a cycle which mechanically repeats itself like the flip of a coin – the fatalistic *as heads is tails* (of the song) philosophy. I have noted the cynical attitude of the Stones already. One such interpretation of this song would be – 'new boss, same as the old boss'.

The rhythm of the song is a fusion of Rock and samba – this latter conjuring up Latin imagery and voodoo/black magic. The "Woo Woo" backing vocal – high pitched and with echo, helps to emphasise the supernatural. Like Johnny Rotten's maniacal laughter, we get Jagger's yelps and grunts in the background before the insistent samba drums get under our skin. The verses, literate, as stated above (who would expect to hear *politesse* on a Rock album?) build to dramatic climax. An unrestrained, swirling, wild guitar break near the end leads to screamed vocals with heavy echo. Another example of not much melody but sensational sound. A throbbing bass adds a deeper dimension as does the boogie woogie piano which takes up the main riff. There are lots of repetition of phrases and short motifs here. One can see why many people believed the influence of the Devil in the words and music.

While a tradition of demon worship in Europe had taken the form of decadent flirtation, the blues in the American south were a more violent occupation. Almost all blues singers, being drifters, were outcasts from the gospel centred communities. "Prodigal Son" by the Rev. Wilkins (a blues singer who reformed and refused to sing anything but religious subjects – hence the blues parable) shows just how seriously the playing of the blues was taken. The Stones welded the two traditions together by "putting on" the Devil and becoming outlaws themselves. In the last chorus of "Jigsaw Puzzle" we find the autobiographical *They've been outcasts all their lives.* We can see that the blues/rock stance taken by the Stones in a different light here.

I think that it will have been quite clear that despite Rotten's condemnation of the Rolling Stones (part of the establishment as he saw it), the two groups as outcasts has a number of similarities. As Burchill & Parsons note;

"The Sex Pistols avoided becoming the Rolling Stones of the 80s with the most constructive move they had made since their formation – disintegration". Perhaps this showed more integrity to the cause of youth rebellion; perhaps they said everything they could in their brief reign as folk-devils; perhaps they wanted the money and run. Whilst the Rolling Stones have become part of the mainstream Rock (as opposed to Pop), in 1968 their targets were as clearly identifiable as those of the Sex Pistols in 1976/77. Their respective stances through their lyrics remain for us all to examine and, to a slightly lesser degree, their music.

BIBLIOGRAPHY

1. Keith Richards "Rolling Stone" Interviews 1967-80 ed P Herbert (1981) Arthur Baker
2. Al Clark (of Virgin Records) in Vermorel (see 21, below)
3. T. Bennett Unit 18 Popular Culture & Hegemony In Post War Britain (1982)
4. Rolling Stones "Our Own Story" (1970) New York
5. Roy Carr (of NME) Sleeve notes Rolled Gold – Rolling Stones (1975)
6. Keith Richards in Dalton (see 10, below)
7. J. Lewis in Vermorel (see 21, below)
8. S. Frith "Sound Effects: Youth, Leisure & The Politics Of Rock (1983) Constable
9. R. Middleton Unit 16 Reading Popular Music (1982)
10. David Dalton "Rolling Stones – The First Twenty Years (1981) Thames & Hudson
11. Keith Richards in Dalton (see 10, above)
12. Jon Landau in Dalton (see 10, above)
13. Dalton (see 10, above)
14. K. Anger in Dalton (see 10, above)
15. S. Frith (see 8, above)
16. Dave Laing "Interpreting Punk Rock" Marxism Today April (1978)
17. D. Hebdige U203 Radio 8 Punk – Subculture & Production
18. D. Hebdige "Subculture: The Meaning Of Style (1982) Methuen
19. L. Hall (of EMI Records) in Vermorel (see 21, below)
20. D. Green (of A & M Records) see Vermorel 21, below)
21. F. & J. Vermorel "Sex Pistols – Inside Story (1981) Star Books

22. J. Burchill & T. Parsons "The Boy Looked At Johnny" (1982) Pluto Press
23. S. Frith (see 8, above)
24. C. Schofield "Jagger" (1983) Methuen

Also useful sources were:

Lou Reed's Velvet Underground "Heroin" 1967 (side B Beggars Banquet tape)
Black Sabbath "Paranoid" 1970 (side A Never Mind... tape)

Additional Bibliography:
J. Muncie U203 Unit 19 Subcultures
J. Muncie & R. Middleton U203 Unit 20 Countercultures
D. Elliot U203 Unit 24 Rock Music Industry
Martin Wright "Jagger & Richards" The Story Of Pop (1973) BBC
Tony Palmer "All You Need Is Love (1976) Futura

Tutor's Verdict: Despite a top A grade it was suggested that I could have looked at the attitude to women and how this was shown in their music. I felt that I was constrained by a word limit, which is perhaps a weak excuse, BUT this could well be a much more detailed and interesting separate undertaking. Watch this space! This book was not bound by any constraints other than those set by myself.

I have finally made reference to this point within the text of the main book with regard to lyrics of a misogynist nature in a number of very famous songs. I was able to set the guidelines by which I have written this and, therefore, had the space and time to address this important issue.

APPENDIX B

ROLLING STONES ALBUMS (These are all in my collection)

First LP (12 x 5)	1964 / 1986
Second LP (Now)	1965 /2002
Aftermath	1966 / 1986
Between The Buttons	1967 / 2002
Flowers	1967 / 1986
Their Satanic Majesties Request	1967 / 1986
Beggars Banquet	1968 / 2002
Let It Bleed	1969 / 1986
Sticky Fingers	1971 / 1986
Sticky Fingers Remastere 2 CD	2009
Sticky Fingers Deluxe + Bonus Tracks	2015
Exile On Main Street	1972
Exile On Main Street Remastered 2 CD	2010
Goats Head Soup	1973
It's Only Rock 'n' Roll	1974
Black & Blue	1976
Some Girls	1978
Some Girls Remastered + Bonus Tracks 2 CD	2011
Emotional Rescue	1980
Tattoo You	1981
Undercover	1983
Dirty Work	1986
Steel Wheels	1989
Voodoo Lounge	1994
Bridges To Babylon	1997
Necrophilia (Bootleg)	2002
Bigger Bang	2005
Music From Charlie Is My Darling 1965	2014
Blue and Lonesome	2016
Goats Head Soup Deluxe 2CD	2020

VINYL

Around and Around (French LP Mono)   1964
Rolling Stones First EP (Mono)   1964

LIVE ALBUMS

Early Sessions (BBC 1963 – 64))   1964
2120 South Michigan Avenue Bootleg   1965
Got Live If You Want It   1966
Live in Hamburg 1965   1965
Live Honolulu   1966
Get Yer Ya-Yas Out   1970
Get Yer Ya-Yas out remastered   1986
Welcome To New York Bootleg   1972
The Great Lost Live Album Bootleg   1972
The Definitive Brussels Affair Bootleg   2CD   1973
Static In The Attic 1974 – 1979 Bootleg 1979
Love You Live   1977
Some Girls Live in Texas   2011
Place Pigalle out takes bootleg   4 CD   1981
San Diego Concert (Brian Matthew) R   1981
Unsurpassed Masters Vols 1 -4 bootleg 4CD 1963 - 71
Unplugged 1968 – 73 Bootleg   1995
Still Life (American Concert1981)   1982
Live All Over The World Bootleg   1989
Wembley July 1990 R 1   1990
Flashpoint   1991
Bright Lights Big City Bootleg   1992
We Want Moore Jagger Bootleg   1992
Miami November 1994 R1   1994
Actin' Strong Bootleg   2 CD   1995
Stripped   1995
St Louis 1997 R 2   1999
No Security   1998
Grande Finale Bootleg 2 CD   1999

Half Stoned Bootleg		2000
Salt & Farewell Bootleg (Twickenh)	2 CD	2003
Live Licks	2 CD	2004
Ottawa 28 August 2005 Bootleg	2 CD	2005
Got To Be Worked On Bootleg		2007
Best of the Bang Bootleg	2 CD	2007
Shine A Light		2008
LA Friday 1975 Live Official Bootleg	2 CD	2012
Live At Tokyo Dome 1990 Official Bootleg	2 CD	2012
Muddy Waters Rolling Stones		2012
Checkerboard Lounge Live		Chicago
Light The Fuse Toronto Live 2005 (Official)		2012
Knebworth 1976 Hot August Night	2 CD	2015
1964 Radio & TV Shows Bootleg		2015
Marquee Club Live in 1971		2015
Live In Leeds (Roundhay Park)	2 CD	2015
Sticky Fingers Live		2015
Totally Stripped Deluxe		2016
No Security San Jose '99	2 CD	2018
Havana Moon	2 CD	2016
Bridges to Bremen	2 CD	2019
Bridges to Buenos Aires	2 CD	2019
Fully Finished Studio Outakes	3 CD	2021
A Bigger Bang: Live on Copacabana Beach	CD	2021
Live at the El Mocambo 1977	2 CD	2022

ASSOCIATED ALBUMS

Jamming With Edward (with Ry Cooder)	1972 / 1995
Rolling Stones Rock n Roll Circus	1996 / 2019

INTERVIEWS

Rolling Stones interviews	1990
Brian Jones interviews 1967	1996

Rolling Stones Loose talk 1964 – 1995		1996
The Sold Stones Stoned Alone 70s – 90s		1996

COMPILATIONS

Hot Rocks 1964 - 71	2 CD	1971
More Hot Rocks		1972
Metamorphosis	1975 /	2002
Rolled Gold	2 LP	1975
Rolled Gold+	2 CD	2007
Made In The Shade		1975
John Peel Stones Retrospective 13 Aug '76		1976
Rewind 1971 - 84		1984
Singles Collection London Years		1989
Jump Back Best of 1971 – 93		1993
Forty Licks	2 CD	2002
Rarities 1971 – 2003 60s UK EP Collection		2005
GRRR!	3 CD	2012
Playing The Blues		2014
Honk	3 CD	2019

SOLO ALBUMS
MICK JAGGER

She's The Boss	1985
Primitive Cool	1987
The Famous Blues Session Bootleg	1992
Through The Years 1982 – 93 Bootleg	1993
Wandering Spirit	1993
Goddess In The Doorway	2001
Alfie Soundtrack with Dave Stewart	2004
Very Best Of …	2007
Super Heavy Deluxe	2011

KEITH RICHARDS

Talk Is Cheap	1988
Main Offender	1992

X-Pensive Winos Live 1988   1991
Vintage Winos   2010
Sure The One You Need Vols. 1 – 3   2009
Crosseyed Heart   2015
Main Offender/ Winos live in London '92 Deluxe 2022
BILL WYMAN
Rhythm Kings Groovin'   2000
Rhythm Kings Double Bill   2 CD   2001
Rhythm Kings Just For A Thrill   2004
A Stone Alone 1974 - 2002   2 CD   2006
Back To Basics   2015
Rhythm Kings Studio Time   2018
RONNIEWOOD
GimmeSomeNeck   1979
Slide On This   1992
Anthology The Essential Crossexion 2CD   2006
I Feel Like Playing   2010
Live At the Ritz (with Bo Diddley)   1988
Mad Lad: A Live Tribute to Chuck Berry   2019
Mr Luck: A Live Tribute to Jimmy Reed   2021
MICK TAYLOR
Montevideo Blues Vol 1 (with Eric Clapton)   1990
A Stones Throw   1999
CHARLIE WATTS
Meets the Danish Radio Big Band   2017
THE NEW BARBARIANS (Wood Richards etc)
Live at Knebworth 11 August '79   1979 / 2015
CHUCK LEAVELL
Back To The Woods   2012
BERNARD FOWLER
Inside Out   2019
BEN WATERS
Boogie 4 Stu (A Tribute to Ian Stewart)   2011
MERRY CLAYTON

Beautiful Scars   2021

TRIBUTE ALBUMS
Stoned Alchemy 27 R' n' B inspirations   1989
Jagger Richards Songbook   1991
Symphonic Music of The Rolling Stones   1994
Paint It Blue Songs of The Stones   1997
Stone Country Country Artists Sing The Stones   1997
Let's Go Get Stoned   2000
Gimme Shelter 16 Covers (Uncut)   2001
Paint It Black Reggae Tribute to The Stones   2002
It's Only Rock n Roll but We Like It   2003
Rolling Stones Songbook Andrew Loog Oldham   1966 / 2004
Blue Roots (My compilation)   2004
Gracias Por El Refugio: 2004
Tributo   Peruano   A   Los   Rolling   Stones
Satisfaction Covers and Cookies   2 CD   2005
The Devil's Jukebox (Uncut)   2005
Bossa n Stones Electro Bossa Songbook   2005
Paint It Black Stones Cover Tracks   2006
Stoned (Mojo) Stones 45th Anniversary   2007
Not Fade Away: 15 Classics Which   2008
Fired   Up   The   Stones
The Roots Of The Rolling Stones (Mojo)   2012
Memory Motel: Inside The World of Keith   2019
Richards (Mojo)
TOTAL ALBUMS   199

RADIO PROGRAMMES (transferred to my Brennan)
Rolling Stones BBC tapes   1963 – 1964
My Top Ten Keith Richards (Andy Peebles Show)
                                           1986
Rolling Stones Interviews: Let's Spend Some Time

                                        1989
Sympathy For The Devil   1989
It's Only Rock n Roll   1989
Charlie   Watts   interview   (Nicky   Campbell)
It's Only Rock n Roll Rolling Stones Story Parts 1/2
Beggars Banquet Keith discusses making of the
1968 album (Roger Scott)   1990
50 What A Drag It Is Getting Old   1992
Jagger at 50   1993
Keith Richards interview (Nicky Campbell)   1993
Jagger: Voodoo Lounge interview   1995
Stones Live 1966 -1994   1995
Bill Wyman in Conversation (Richard Allinson)
Station To Station   1995
Brian Jones Dream Of Life BBC R2   1999
Charlie Watts Stone Alone   1999
Growing Old Disgracefully   2002
Rolling Stones Story Parts 2 & 3 (Bob Harris)   2002
Rolling Stones (Steve Wright interviews)   2003
Real Wild Child Jagger / Richards Glimmer Twins
                                        2003
Rock's Back Pages   2004
Rolling Stones (Janice Long Interviews)   2005
Like The Rolling Stones Part 1   2005
Like The Rolling Stones Part 2   2005
Still Live Retrospective of past year   2006
4 x 4 Rolling Stones Talk About Each Other   2006
TOTAL RADIO PROGRAMMES 29

OFFICIAL DVDs (Documentary and Concert footage)
Stones in the Park   1970 / 2006
Sympathy For The Devil   1968 / 2004
Four Flicks   4 DVD   2003
Toronto Rocks   2004

Get Yer Ya Yas Out		2005
Big Hits (High Tide Green Grass)		2006
Live at the Max		2006
The Biggest Bang	4 DVD	2007
Shine A Light		2008
Ladies & Gentlemen		2010
The Biggest Bang		2010
T A M I Show 1964 (NTSC)		2010
Rare & Unseen		2010
Stones in Exile		2010
Some Girls Live (Texas) 1978		2011
Under Review 1975 – 83		2012
Muddy Waters Rolling Stones		2012
Checkerboard Lounge Chicago		1981
Hampton Coliseum Live 1981		2014
Knebworth Fair 1976		2015
Under Review 1975 – 83		2012
Sweet Summer Sun (Hyde Park)		2013
Marquee Club Live in 1971		2015
Live In Leeds (Roundhay Park)		2015
Sticky Fingers Live		2015
Totally Stripped Deluxe		2016
No Security San Jose '99		2018
Havana Moon		2016
Rolling Stones Rock n Roll Circus		1996 / 2019
Bridges to Bremen		2019
Bridges to Buenos Aires '98		2019
A Bigger Bang Live on Copacabana Beach 2 DVD		
		2021

TOTAL OFFICIAL DVDs 38

BOOTLEG DVDs

Cocksucker Blues 1972	2003
Keith Richards & The New Barbarians	2007

The Mick Taylor	VHS	2010
Great Video Hits		1986
Voodoo Lounge Concert		1995
Bridges To Babylon Tour extracts		1998

APPENDIX C
PITCHFORK: THE MOST TRUSTED VOICE IN MUSIC (AN ONLINE AMERICAN MUSIC MAGAZINE)

THE BEST ROLLING STONES SONGS THAT DON'T REALLY SOUND LIKE THE ROLLING STONES

by Stuart Berman   April 22, 2019

"I'd Much Rather Be With the Boys" (1964)

Appears on: The rarities collection *Metamorphosis*
The closest the Stones ever got to sounding like: the Ronettes

While pretty much every Stones original carries the Jagger-Richards imprimatur, this 1964 outtake is credited to Richards and the band's first manager, Andrew Loog-Oldham. Though it's sung from the perspective of a guy who prefers to hang out with his pals over his date, "I'd Much Rather Be With the Boys" sounds tailor-made for an innocent girl group, complete with a Spector-sized backbeat and high-pitched harmonies that waft through the song like a gentle breeze. Feeling it was a touch too off-brand for a band with a nasty reputation to uphold, the Stones handed the song off to fellow Brit beat combo the Toggery Five (whose version changed the chorus to "I'd rather be out with the boys," reportedly to defuse the original's homoerotic undertones). A half-century later, the song finally found its rightful home when Ronnie Spector covered it (as "I'd Much Rather Be With the Girls") for her 2016 album *English Heart*.

"We Love You" (1967)

Appears on: *Singles Collection: The London Years*
The closest the Stones ever got to sounding like· psycho
delic Beatles

The Stones' relationship with psychedelia was, to put
it mildly, complicated. Though their 1967 album *Their
Satanic Majesties Request* has held up better than its sec-
ond-rate-*Sgt.-Pepper* reputation suggests, the Stones
never made for the most convincing hippies; check out
Mick's thoroughly unenthused "I can't believe my mom
dressed me as a wizard for Halloween" look on the album's front cover. Their brief flower-power flirtation did
yield a few eternal classics, the most underrated of which
is this non-album single from the summer of '67. Recorded while Mick and Keith were embroiled in an infamous drug-arrest scandal, "We Love You" is psychedelia
dripping with cynicism. They clang jail-cell doors and
turn hippy-dippy platitudes into sneering taunts directed
at the police and prosecutors. With the song's needling
piano line, buzzing mellotrons, thundering drums, and
ecstatic harmonies (courtesy of an uncredited John Lennon and Paul McCartney) all sucked into a cyclonic swirl,
"We Love You" is essentially the Stones' "Tomorrow
Never Knows." (Also check "Jumpin' Jack Flash" B-side
"Child of the Moon," aka the Stones' "Rain.")

"I Just Want to See His Face" (1972)

Appears on: *Exile on Main St.*
The closest the Stones ever got to sounding like: gospel as remixed by Lee "Scratch" Perry

The Stones' 1972 double-album messterpiece was born in a heroin-induced haze of glamor and squalor, as the Stones hid out from the taxman in the dank basement of Keith's French Riviera mansion, letting the tape roll into the wee hours. Amid *Exile*'s burnt-spoon blend of blues, country, soul, and rockabilly, the uncanny "I Just Want to See His Face" raises you from the moldy cellar like a fleeting out-of-body experience. It's ostensibly a church hymn, but one whose murky, mercurial production and warbling electric-piano tones make it sound like it was surreptitiously recorded at Sunday service through a pocket dial.

"Winter" (1973)

Album: *Goats Head Soup*
The closest the Stones ever got to sounding like: *Astral Weeks*

Arriving after one of the most hallowed four-album runs in rock history, *Goats Head Soup* revealed the first chink in the Stones' armor, showing early signs of the aesthetic power struggle between trendspotting and traditionalism that's played out on pretty much every Stones record since. But the divine "Winter" exists in a universe all its own. Though seemingly cut from the same cloth as strung-out ballads like "Moonlight Mile" and "Wild Horses," it possesses a celestial aura and stream-of-consciousness drift that elevates it to an astral plane the Stones would never strive toward again.

"Time Waits for No One" (1974)

Appears on: *It's Only Rock 'n Roll*
The closest the Stones ever got to sounding like: It's tempting to say Santana, but the iconic "Can't You Hear Me Knocking" already pulled off that trick more blatantly, so let's go with "tropicália Steely Dan."

Though he was a member of the Stones for less than 10 percent of their existence, guitarist Mick Taylor was a crucial contributor to the band's early-'70s canon, with soulful solos that brought a greater degree of melodic sophistication and emotional depth to even their raunchiest rockers. This Brazilian-spiced standout from the otherwise workmanlike *It's Only Rock 'n Roll*, Taylor's final album as a Stone, serves as a fitting epitaph for his brief but fruitful tenure in the band. The Stones could always jam with the best of 'em, but Taylor's graceful extended fretboard workout pushes them to uncharted realms of psych-jazz improvisation.

"Shattered" (1978)

Appears on: *Some Girls*
The closest the Stones ever got to sounding like: *Neu! 75*

"Shattered" is probably the most well-known Stones song included here, making regular appearances on past compilations and set lists. But that doesn't make it any less of a bizarre anomaly in their canon. The song was famously part of the Stones' response to punk, but in contrast to fellow *Some Girls* aggressors like "Lies" and "Respectable," it doesn't rock in a typically trashy garage-band fashion. Rather, the dry, vacuum-sealed production and relentless motorik minimalism of "Shattered" stake the middle ground between CBGB and the Autobahn, while the band's stoner-doo-wop backing vocals goad Jagger into the most hysterical performance of his career. (For more quality Stones-on-punk snarl, check out *Emotional Rescue*'s "Where the Boys Go," in which Mick goes full Pete Shelley.)

"Dance (Pt. 1)" (1980)

Appears on: *Emotional Rescue*
The closest the Stones ever got to sounding like: peak hour at the Paradise Garage

If the Stones' 1978 club crossover hit "Miss You" was the sound of Mick cooly slinking into the discotheque at sunset, the more intoxicated "Dance Pt. 1" finds him still on the floor several hours later, soaked in sweat, grinding his teeth, and jabbering nonsense into random strangers' ears.

"Heaven" (1981)

Appears on: *Tattoo You*
The closest the Stones ever got to sounding like: chill wave

While *Tattoo You* marked the Stones' exile from beat street, the album's ballad-heavy second side still gave Jagger plenty of opportunities to flex his smooth falsetto for a slow dance. Amid the canon of mellow Stones songs, none are as strange and sublime as "Heaven." Atop a featherweight snare-rim rhythm, Jagger's eerily airy voice blurs into a vapor trail of guitar lines and wind-chimed mysticism, yielding a song that's as alluring and ambiguous as a desert mirage.

"Too Much Blood" (1983)

Appears on: *Undercover*
The closest the Stones ever got to sounding like: an Arthur Russell 12-inch

Intimations of violence were always baked into the Stones' most powerful songs, but as their music got slicker and more streamlined, their attempts at provocation became more flagrant—and, in some cases, more laughable. "Too Much Blood" has the distinction of boasting both Jagger's most cringe-worthy vocal turn (in the form of a spoken-word freestyle about cannibalistic serial killers and *Texas Chainsaw Massacre* hot takes) and one of the Stones' most hypnotic grooves—a strobe-lit, proto-house pulse that cranked up the cowbell-clanking freakiness even more in Arthur Baker's companion dub remix.

"Almost Hear You Sigh" (1989)

Appears on: *Steel Wheels*
The closest the Stones ever got to sounding like: yacht rock

Even the most committed Stones fan has to concede that the band's catalog stopped feeling vital from the mid-1980s onward, as they settled into their role as elder statesmen of the stadium circuit and released increasingly sporadic albums. To the group's credit, they resisted the slide into syrupy dentist-office pop that knee-capped many of their fellow '60s-rock survivors during the '80s. However, this sleek mid-tempo ballad from the better-than-you-might-remember *Steel   Wheels* suggests an adult-contemporary Stones might not have been such a bad thing. With its glassy piano strokes, new-agey acoustic picking, and shoulder-rubbing "ooh ooh oohs," "Almost Hear You Sigh" is just begging for a cover by Bon Hornsby.

APPENDIX D

The following is the list of the DVDs that I have made with briefly noted contents. It is in no set order other than the order in which it has been put together, though there is the basis of a chronological thread to be seen. There are, also, for the keen eyed observer, just one or two programmes that have been repeated which is completely down to me forgetting that I have already recorded or downloaded the item. There a few items recorded from German TV. I have found that the Blues scene in Germany is very strong. An example of this concerns Miller Anderson, the ex- Keef Hartley Band singer and guitarist who I have long admired, I was able to meet with him and had a long chat with at a Colin Hodgkinson Steaming Blues event courtesy of the Nene Valley Railway at Wansford, Peterborough. His solo records are now via a German company from where he is very well supported. But I digress.

Here is the list:

Gimme Shelter 1970 World in Action Jagger interview
1968 Old Grey Whistle Test interview   VH1 Hits

Dick Taylor on MJ Hero 2 Hero Ronnie & Charlatans
Drugs Bust ITN News   Bigger Bang Tour (Newsnight)

Let's Spend the Night Together 1982   J'Accuse 1990
25 x 5: Continuing Adventures 1989   MTV Tracks

David Hepworth vids/i/vs Voodoo Lounge set design
Jump Back   Urban Jungle Tour The Hits MTV Awards
X-Pensive Winos in92 Reggae & Country Mick Taylor

on German TV   Voodoo Lounge Europe Live   More Hits
Live in Barcelona   1990   Voodoo Lounge Live 1994
Stripped: Studio & Live performances   2005

Keith interview 96   Satisfaction 20 Years On   Work Five
Years, Twenty Years Hanging Around '89   X-Pensive
Winos   Jerry Hall: Ten of the Best   Rhythms of the
World 1989
Jagger/Richards/Wood Tracks Brit Girls Marianne Faith
full   Stones Day videos/interviews   In Russia   Pop Up
 Vids   Egos & Icons 97   Bill Wyman Rhythm Kings 98
Sticky Fingers   Jagger Centre (German TV) Millennium
 Song 2000

TFI Rolling Stones Chris Evans in Chicago 99   Back to
Babylon 99   TOTP Special   Close Up (Marianne) Voo
doo Lounge Special   MTV interviews   Hit Tracks   Stones
in   S. America

VH1 Fashion Awards   VH1 Hits Brit Girls (Marianne)
Bridges to Babylon Tour   Waiting on a Friend Pop Up
CNN Stones on Tour (age)   BBC/ITN Divorce 98/99   Ed
 Sullivan   Album Charts   Fame, Set & Match   Mick at
Cricket '02   Mick at the Awards   Ron/Lily Savage   Ron
at the Brits 2000

Rock'n'Roll Myths (Redlands)   Rise of Celebrity Class
Mick's Girls   04   Ronnie Wood   South Bank Show 04

Being Mick '01 Ron on Jonathan Ross '01 Sir Mick '02
Jagger Ultimate Performer Mick n Keef on Simpsons 03
The One & Only Rolling Stones 03   TOTP2 Special '03
Sympathy for the Devil (remix) 2003

Super Bowl 06 Bill on Archaeology and Cartoons
Summer of Love - Bill & Mandy Beatles v Stones/Drugs
60s Decade Final TOTP- "Last Time"/ Keef on TOTP -
Inside Story Hampden Concert 06 (audio only) Greatest
Rio Concert -Albums - Exile/Let it Bleed Greatest Gigs
 Hyde Park

Who Killed The Rolling Stone - Life & Death of Brian
Jones (Inside John Peel's Record Box)

Isle of Wight Festival '06 extracts   Ron on Sky TV '07
"Ready Steady Go" Stones Live Jagger at Live Aid 85
Stones Tour 1989/90   "Shine A Light" premiere

Hail Hail Rock n Roll (film)/ Millennium Top Artistes(14)
Video Rewind(uncensored)/Voodoo Lounge Official Tour
Vid / Castrol preview of Bridges to Babylon Tour
Jerry Wexler on The Stones - Extracts fom unreleased
Charlie is My Darling - Julien Temple on Undercover vid
Sounds of the 60s - TOTP 1967 - Pop Go the 60s '69
Jagger i/v w David Dimbleby 71 - Ronnie Wood on Later
2000 Renault advert (I'm Free) Greek TV 2006 - Carlo
Little on Littlejohn: Loud and Unleashed 9 June 1998

Exile of the Stones (R2 documentary) Mick Jagger on
 Huey Morgan Show 6Music//Jagger's Jukebox (R2)

Mick Jagger on Larry King Show May 2010 (no ads)
Shine A Light (Scorsese Documentary)Greek Subtitles
Altamont Footage/American Idol 2010 Stones Night
Guitar Heroes Johnny Winter- Jumping Jack Flash/
Stones in Exile (documentary on making of Exile on
Street/A Bigger Bang Concert from Rio de Janeiro 2006

Pirates of the Caribbean 3(KR extract) - Can Blue Men Sing the Whites (BW & KR) Jagger at Grammys '11 - Bleu de Chanel ad - Truth & Lies (doc) // At Home with Keith Richards (Paul Sexton i/v) Radio2 AUDIO only

Rock n Roll Grew Up / Live Aid clips/ Stones in Beatles Decade/Drugs Bust/Ronnie on the One Show(17/9/10) Truth & Lies(doc)Keith on Andrew Marr Show (Oct '10) 24 Oct 2010 KR on Culture Show BBC2 (28 Oct '10)

The First Time w Charlie /The Stones by the Stones (Paul Sexton i/v) BBC6// Johnny Walker reviews Some Girls album/ Jagger Richards Songwriters (ALL audio)

Brown Sugar w Tina Turner 88 /Love Hurts KR w Norah Jones/Shattered Trabendo 2012/ Sympathy FTD 98 Beast of Burden/Bigger Bang Toronto05/ Bridges2 Bab ylon Berlin 98 Midnight Rambler MSG 03/Monkey Man Everybody Needs Somebody Paris 03/ One More Shot 12/ salt of the Earth 07Shine A Light w Bonnie Raitt 06 Under My Thumb Leeds 82Time waits For No One/ Rolling Stones at the BBC/...sings The Rolling Stones

Concert Footage 64 (TV)/ Marquee Club71/ Barcelona 90/Stripped 95/ Toronto Phoenix 05 plus select tracks // 50 &Counting O2 Arena Nov 2012 (YouTube footage) Crossfire Hurricane (2 pts) 2012/Charlie Is My Darling 65 KR performances (solo & w Winos) KR i/vs/ Charlie i/vs Ron Wood performances & i/vs/ Rolling Stones at 50

Mick & Keith concert for NYC/ Hard Woman (MJ) Mick & Tina Live Aid/ On Your Way To School (early demo) Rice Krispies ads(2 versions)/ Mercedes Ad./ Shanghai Midnight Rambler Wild Horses// Greek TV ad-GRRR!

Who Killed A Rolling Stone?/ Shenandoah (KR & Tom
Waits 50 & Counting Tour News/ Pat Andrews w Brian's
son Stones' i/vs / Brian i/v Monterey Pop 67 & Jan 68
Jimi Hendrix w Brian - My Little One / Brian's Death: My
Legends The Truth/ Confidential / Stones TAMI Show 64

50 & Counting Tour...USA 2013 Staples Center LA
50 & Counting Stones Guest Artistes May - June 2103
Mick Taylor Taj Mahal John Fogerty Bonnie Raitt Keith
Urban Taylor Swift Tom Waits Gwen Stefani John Mayer
Gary Clark Dave Grohl Katy Perry

Jagger The One Show (Nov2012) Sky News ITV Mick
& Keith Somerset House July '12 ABC News Lennon &
Jagger Blind Leading the Blind Jagger Guitar (Brown
 Sugar) Evening Gown JJ Flash Jagger/Springsteen
(Satisfaction) Old Habits Die Hard Party Doll Perform
ance/Hyde Park 69   Visions Of Paradise Facebook (50 &
Counting)
Can Feel Your Fire Satisfaction Miracle Worker-Super
Heavy) Wild Horses MJ Australasian Tour Melbourne
1988(with Joe Satriani)

 Early Years Songs & Vids: Come On It Should Be You
King Bee Little By Little Around & Around Chess
Chicago Outtakes 64 The Last Time Satisfaction Paint
It Black Oh Baby Mother's Little Helper We Love You
Heart Of Stone She Said Yeah Stray Cat Blues Flight
505 Good Times Good Times, Bad Times Talkin' 'bout
You Lady Jane She's A Rainbow Citadel Concerts of
67 Weird Moments
The Later Years: 50 & Counting. Headlining At Glaston
bury selected pre and post festival extras

Voodoo Lounge Tour Giants Stadium NJ August 1994
Montreal 1964 Paris 65-67 Good Time Women Satis
faction (Brittany Howard) Beast Of Burden (Bette Midler
Montage Of Stones' Music in Film Shine A Light
Rehearsal, Trailers, Reviews w Martin Scorsese Time
Waits For No One Tribute Shine A Light

Rolling Stones Songs Featured In TV Advertising (from
Rice Krispies 1964) to Present (2013)
Mick & Keith on OGWT 1972   Keith on OGWT 1974
Google Play mini docs (x 2) with Mick & Keith Talking
About Previous Tours The Rolling Stones Backstage 76
On Fire In 2014 Australian TV Interview

The Rolling Stones Just For The Record 60s & 70s
 Rolling Stones Just For The Record 2002 & Beyond
Till The Next Goodbye MJ at the White House
featuring Jeff Beck, Buddy Guy BB King etc and Pres.
Obama 2012

Versions of Little Red Rooster: Rolling Stones Howlin'
Wolf Willie Dixon Arno Bernard Fowler Eric Clapton
Canned Heat Etta James Fabulous Fleetwoods Junior
 Wells Keith Richards Kenny Wayne Shepherd Kevin
Borich Layla Zoe Guy Davis Taj Mahal Otis Rush/ Rollin
Stones Tom Waits Car Wash Billy Branch Luther
 Allison Robben Ford Savoy Brown Blue Riders Big
 Mama Thornton Two Riders Persuasions Sugar Blue
Lucky Peterson MIck Taylor Super Super Blues Band
Jesus & Mary Chain

Christopher Bruce's Ballet - Rooster celebrating music
of Rolling Stones feat. Little Red Rooster, Paint It Black
Play With Fire, As Tears Go By, Not Fade Away, Sym

pathy For The Devil, Ruby Tuesday & Lady Jane
Pathe News:The Rolling Stones - Gather No Moss 64
Receive Award On The Thames 1965 Arrive Sydney 65
Arrive In Sydney For Another Tour 1966 Freed 1967
Concert 1969 On Stage 1970 Sing Satisfaction 1970
The Second Wave 1962-69 (full movie) 2011

Tour Announcements: New York 1975 Stockholm 1975
Steel Wheels 1989 Juilliard 2005 Superbowl 2006 Tip
of The Tongue 2007 On Fire 2014 Singapore 2014
No Security Tour, North America compilation 1999
Palais Royale, Toronto 16 August 2002

Full Concert Newark, New Jersey 15 December 2012
Pay Per View TV broadcast)
Rolling Stones 14 On Fire Tour.Macau, China 9 March
2014 Amateur YouTube footage

Sticky Fingers Live Video History of the Stones Top
Ten Rolling Stones Moments Miss You (live 97) Silver
Train (Nostalgienacht)'76/'86 Moonlight Mile Tumbling
Dice (Rio, Lisbon '14 w Springsteen) Biggest Mistake
The Greatest Band In The History Of The World
14onFire Tour Rehearsals and Performances Abu Dhabi
Tokyo Tour Of Asia Oslo European Leg Cover Versions:
Betty La Vette - Salt Of The Earth John Mayer - Beast
of Burden Joan Jett/Slash - Star Star Jagger Clips Jon
Bon Jovi Funny Story Jagger Interview on "60 Minutes"
Python Promo James Brown Biopic "Get On Up" Promo

Selection Happy Birthday Tributes To Mick Jagger On
65th -71st Birthdays US News Item on Jagger's Age
Jagger & Richards OGWT 1972 Jagger on OGWT 1973
Jagger Interview "Raw & Uncut" 1985 MTV Jagger

Interview 1993
Rolling Stones Milan 10-1-71 Ladies & Gentlemen..It's
The Rolling Stones Dead Flowers (official Vid) Keith &
Willie Nelson Dead Flowers Keith/Sheryl Crow Happy
99 Keith & Friends Wild Horses Keith's Tribute To Bob
Marley Words Of Wonder/Get Up, Stand Up

Get On Up - James Brown Biopic produced by Jagger
Interviews, Trailers and Reviews. Interviews and Reviews
from US TV shows.Official trailers.James Brown singing
It's A Man's, Man's, Man's World (1967)
Beast of Burden. Rolling Stones and cover versions feat
Bette Midler, The Kooks, Jess Greenberg, John Mayer,
Juliette Lewis, Pete Herger, Colbie Caillet, Lee De Wyze
Bruce Springsteen and Alejandro Escovedo, Buckwheat
Zydeko, Joan Osborne, Katy Perry, Rockin' Dopsie Jr.,
The Hives, Lifehouse, Jessica Meuse & Caleb Johnson.

Great Keith I / vs: Punk Music K R's Guitar Chops
Fan Pirates of Caribbean clip Family Robin Williams
impression Rich Branson Dishes The Dirt *You Think
You Know The Rolling Stones Simpson's Clip Two
Cellos Satisfaction Jagger Interview (Paula Yates) Don't
Stop Highwire Rough Justice Mixed Emotions Time Is
On My Side Terrifying Rock & A Hard Place Undercover
Of The Night Where Boys Go The Rolling Stones Live
Essen10 Oct 70 Live Madison Square Garden 25 July
1972 Star Star 1975

Jagger Richards Interviews KR: Dirty Work 86 Paul
Shaffer Friday Night Video 86 Famous Last Words 60
Minutes Rewind - Not Fade Away Bigger Bang 05 MJ:
Peter Tosh 78 Paula Yates 82 The Tube 83 The Raw
(Uncut) Rutles Outtakes Famous Last Words 91 James

Brown & Get On Up" Film 14 Ron Wood: Jools Holland i/v 07 Andre Marr

Stones vs Beatles: Music B vs RS (Australian TV Show) Live RnR Shootout I Wanna Be Your Man Drift Away Lennon & Jagger 68 JL intro to J J. Flash KR Remembers JL Stones Imitating Beatles (Lennon) Rivalry Myth (Ringo & Charlie) MJ Inducts Beatles To Rock n Roll Hall of Fame Stones Sing Mock Beatles 65 They Sold Their Souls Mash Ups: Drive My Start/ Sym pathy Friends Ladies & Gents'72 Tour Viet Nam War: Paint It Black Gimme Shelter (Huey Helicopter) Sym pathy for The Devil   If You Can Rock Me

Simon Wells Radio i/vs on "Butterfly On A Wheel" The Great Rolling Stones Drugs Bust. 1 With Rod Quinn of ABC Radio (5 March 2012) 2 With Tony Peters of Icon fetch 10 April 2012. News Clips and Features on Raid Chichester Trial of Mick and Keith in 1967. Plus We Love You (Official Video) and I'm Free Video

MJ Interviews Ireland 65 1966 Close Up 68 1970 1972 OGWT73 Eliot Mintz 73 Newsnight 81 The Tube 83 Live Aid 85 Primitive Cool 88 Fiona Phillips 93 Wan dering Spirit 93 Enigma 01 Alfie 04 Song writing 07 Shine A Light 2008

Controversial 78 Very Best of Mick J 07 MJ x Tortoise Matsumoto 08 CNN Drugs, Critics 10 NBC 12 James Brown Film 14 Get On Up Premier 14 Simon Mayo 14 Letterman 10 Things'14 60 Minutes(Australia)'14 Death of L'Wreen Scott 15 Wives & Lovers'15 Funniest 1/vs15 I/v Highlights 15 Noel Gallagher: Bowie or Jagger 15

Announcement of Latin American Tour 2016 Jagger tourist Concert extracts from Argentina, Chile, Peru &

Mexico   Preps for Cuba Free Concert   News Media
Reaction Concert extracts and crowd reaction
Stones concert Maracana Stadium Rio de Janeiro 20
Feb 2016 (mainly unofficial YouTube footage)

Videos Rare and Familiar-Around & Around Carol You
Better Move On Little Red Rooster Play With Fire Satis
faction The Last Time Time Is On My Side   Down The
Road Apiece Lady Jane Fortune Teller Out Of Time
Under the Boardwalk 19th Nervous Breakdown Dandel
ion We Love You Have You Seen Your Mother Ruby
Tuesday Under My Thumb I Am Waiting Cry To Me
Paint It Black Child Of The Moon She's A Rainbow
Love in Vain Salt Of The Earth Jumpin' Jack Flash
Country Honk Gimme Shelter Parachute Woman Dead
Flowers Wild Horses Beast Of Burden Star Star
Can't Always Get What You Want Sympathy
Exhibitionism: Announcements, interviews & news clips
about Rolling Stones Exhibition in London. It features
the Stones themselves & the world's media
Keith & Stuff: Origin of the Species BBC doc. Year by
Year 1963-2015 Keith at 71 Andrew Marr Show (Cross-
eyed Heart 2015) Jimmy Fallon Tonight Show Love
Overdue Fronting documentary weekend Sept 2015
\BBC 4 Eileen

The Rolling Stones Live at the Saitama Super Stadium
2 April 2006 (Bigger Bang Tour)
The Rolling Stones Live at The Desert Trip Festival
Empire Polo Club, Indio CA USA 7 October 2015

Ask Keith Question & Answer Session: Composing
Writing, Writing with others, instruments played, working with Ronnie & Mick Taylor. Lost Weekend, Julien

Temple, Tour of USA, inspirations, Crosseyed Heart album, Gus & Me book

Bill Wyman 80th Birthday Blues Fest 29 Oct 2016: Guests, Bob Geldoff, Mick Hucknall, Robert Plant, Steve Van Zandt, Mark Knopfler. Je Suis Un Rock Star, Rhythm Kings tracks: Baby Please Don't Go, Chicken Shack Boogie, You Never Can Tell, Green River, Melody. Stones song In Another Land, Ask Keith: Bill's Bass playing

The Rolling Stones: Just For The Record 1960s, 1970s and 1980s documentaries
The Rolling Stones Just For The Record 1990s, 2000 and Beyond documentaries (no actual Rolling Stones music played)

Brown Sugar, Out of Control (both Havana) Desert Trip Announcement, Little T & A Like A Rolling Stone (with Dylan), Satisfaction, Jumpin Jack Flash Midnight Rambler, Gimme Shelter (Las Vegas) 2000 Light Years/Sympathy Billionaires Party Start Me Up/Bitch Tumbling Dice Private Show plus more Boston extracts Country Honk Commit A Crime Ride em On Down What the Stones have learned From Each Other Over 50 Years Reaction to Trump victory Latin American Tour 2016 Announcement & Teaser Trailer Stones in Chile Santiago Concert Paint It Black (Argentina) Keith ovation La Plata Argentina, Maracana (Brazil) Full Concert Jagger in Bogota The Stones in Mexico Cuba prepares Jagger makes way for Obama Cuba goes crazy for the Stones, Havana Rocks Stones play to i.2 million in Cuba

Blue & Lonesome announcement w TV ad MJ on BBC

TV breakfast show Chuck Leavell on Stones album (Fox News) Jagger in Amsterdam Mick n Keith on the Blues Commit A Crime (White House)Just Your Fool Ride 'em On Down(both Desert Trip)Kirsten Stewart- Ride 'em On Down (off. Video) Blue & Lonesome Hoo Doo Blues Hate To See You Go I Can't Quit You Baby Little Rain All Of Your Love Everybody Knows About My Good Thing Just Like I treat You Jagger answers tweets Jagger Interview with Luciana Gimenez (Brazil)
Full Concert Perth Australia Nov 2014 14 On Fire Tour

VINYL TV Series:Jagger & Scorsese Trailers & i/vs Scorsese & the use of The Rolling Stones music in his films
Keith & Ronnie interviews Blue and Lonesome w Becko from Triple M Sydney Stones VH 1 Special 1994 Story of The Rolling Stones (biog) Rolling Stones 2nd Wave

Bill Wyman interviews 1960s - 2015 Wyman on the 60s Bill & Charlie Sweden 1965 USA 1960s 1972 Rapido i/v 1974 OGWT 1882 Kenny Everett Show! 985 Late Night Show 1990 Interview 1998 Oslo 2000 Jules Holland on Later 2003 Dutch TV 2005 Dave Lawrence Radio Show 2013 Me 1 interview 2015 Mark Bright 2015 Back To Basics 2015 Dartford Plaque tirade Fromage ou Dessert The Rolling Stones First Night Back Tokyo Dome Bunkyo, Tokyo from the 14 On Fire Tour -Full concert

Keith transformation 1962-2016 KR 1969 KR 1973 Melbourne Blow Blues/Boudoir Stomp/Heart of Stone Top6 Wives/Lovers KR/Uschi Maier Secret of long marriage KR with family   Keith: Friday nights parts 1 & 2 KR at Apollo Gimme Shelter With Eric Clapton Goin' Down Slow KR & Ronnie Road Trip Premiere Ask Keith:1 Do

You Play Banjo 2 Use of guitar foot pedal 3 Blues solo Album? 4 Blues Album Stones Super Bowl Half time prep 1972 Unofficial footage w Stevie Wonder Bulldog- T & A forerunner She Was Hot -original country version Jagger Mini Biog Jagger transformation 18-73 Moves Like Jagger At 69 MJ Lifestyle Secret Love Letters Net Worth 2017 Moves Like Jagger Maroon 5 Videos Of Dance Moves -Start Me Up/ Ain't |Too Proud To Beg Crazy Mama/Goin' To A Go Go/Hang Fire/Hey Negrita/ Hot Stuff/ Too Much Blood Rip This Joint Terrifying of 2 political songs England Lost (w lyrics) & Get A Grip remix by Kevin Parker/Amok/ Matt Clifford/ Seeb

No Filter Tour Hamburg 2017: Announcement & Prep Sound Checks Hotel 5 questions (auf Deutsch) High- lights - Sympathy, Tumbling Dice, Out of Control, Just Your Fool, Play With Fire, You Can't Always Get What You Want, Dancing With Mr D, Under My Thumb Paint It Black, Honky Tonk Women, Slipping Away, Midnight Rambler, Street Fighting Man, Brown Sugar, Satisfact ion Gimme Shelter, Jumpin' Jack Flash, Departure from Hamburg
The Rolling Stones No Filter Tour 2017 Full Concert Hamburg Stadtpark Festwiese 9 September 2017

Ronnie Wood: Wives and Lovers The Faces 1969-75 Book Andrew Marr Show 2013 The One Show 2015 Talks drugs & Keith jamming With Mick Taylor: Baby What Do You Want Me To Do/Live/I'm Mr Luck/Goin' Upside Your Head/ Big Boss Man/ Shame Shame Shame Happy 100th Birthday Aunt Mary Art Book Signing New Channel on YouTube Reveals Cancer Scare Discusses Cancer Battle The One Show Elvis Presley Tribute 2017

Best of "No Filter" Tour 2017: Sympathy (Arnhem) Tum
bling Dice(Stockholm) Just Your Fool(Munich) Ride 'em
On Down (Paris) Dancing With Mr D (Zurich) She's A
Rainbow (Spielberg) Play With Fire(Hamburg) She's So
Cold (Paris) You Can't Always Get What You Want
(Zurich) Street Fighting Man (Arnhem) Start Me Up
(Lucca) Brown Sugar (Stockholm) Jumpin' Jack Flash
(Dusseldorf) PLUS Concert from Barcelona 27 Sept
2017 (Estadi Olimpic)

The Rolling Stones Croke Park Dublin 17 May 2018:
Stones arrive in Dublin Rehearsals Sympathy Paint It
Black Just Your Fool Ride 'em On Down Neighbours
Wild Horses You Can't Always Get.... Honky Tonk
Women Before They Make Me Run The Worst Miss
You Midnight Rambler Jumpin' Jack Flash Brown
Sugar Gimme Shelter Satisfaction
Rolling Stones Manchester Old Trafford 5 June 2018
Jumpin Jack Flash Tumbling Dice Just Your Fool Let's
Spend The Night Together Like A Rolling Stone You
Can't Always get.. Paint It Black Honky Tonk Women
You Got The Silver Sympathy Miss You (London Gig)
Midnight Rambler Start Me Up Gimme Shelter Satis-
Faction PLUS Richard Ashcroft

Rolling Stones in commercials and trailers 1964 - 2018
75 examples from different countries (UK, USA, Japan,
Europe and the Middle East) Full list inside Wide range
of tracks covered inc. She's A Rainbow, Satisfaction
Sympathy For The Devil Start Me Up etc. Feature film
trailers. Tours and tour info plus individual record plugs
and various commercial products
Another 50 commercials and trailers from around the
world including Australia and Brazil AND featuring the

famous 1964 Rice Krispies advert

COMMERCIALS and Trailers 64 -18 94JHJY spot Sympathy; 1980 Bally Pinball
Machine;Small Circle of Friends (Trailer); Beggars Banquet (50 anniv); Stones in
Exile; Acuna - Rainbow; AppleMac Colours; Banco de Chile x 2; banned corvette
Hyde Park 69; Beer Run; Bent (Trailer); Brown Sugar; Budwiser Start Me Up; Call
Of Duty Black Ops; C8 promo; Cold Case Almost Paradise & Shattered; Coca
Cola Brasil 06; Commercial; Desert Trip; Eau Savage; ESPN Football; Las Vegas
Exhibitionism; Fallen, Fear (Trailers); Gap khakis; George Piliouras; Gimme
Shelter
Goats Head Soup; IORR ; upoutavka; Hertog Jan 09; Insignia; IMAX; Starsearch;
MTV; Joy (DIOR), Ladies & Gentlemen; Groupies; Lexmark; LOL trailer; Mayans:
Mesrine L'instinct de Mort; Miami Medical; Jagger; Money Desert;
Motorola:Neogam
New Fit; Zip Code Tour; Superbowl 08; Nissan; Not Fade Away; O Heart; Omega;

Shine A Light (Trailer); La Retrospective; 40 Licks Tour; TDK IORR; Czech Republic
Brown Sugar; Argentina; NBA Promo; Sam Cutler; Satisfaction; Scotch Tape 85; Se
Drogas e Rolling Stones; Sexy Jeans; Stones in Exile trailer; Rice Krispies; Snicker
Bernard Fowler; Stri of Echoes trailer; Stoned; Superbowl XLI; Biggest Bang; Cave
50th anniversary; The Family tralier; The Righteous Kill trailer; Music Scene;
Adelaide;
Charkie Is Y Darling; Confessin The Blues x 2; Crossfire Hurricane trailer; GRRR!
Rolled
Gold; Sticky Fingers Fonda Theatre; Biggest bang DVD; Vinyl Unboxing; Voodoo
Lounge
trailer; 50th anniv concert; 2007 German Tour; announce 2019 US tour; On Air; Son
bookmit Noten; Stripped; Copacobabna 06; Worlds End trailer; 60 minutes; T-Home
Godard Sympathy; UFC on Fox; VH1 Mick; VW Golf; Wall Street trailer; One More

Part of the DVD cover showing the list of adverts the Stones music
has been used in. They cover a wide range of products and are
from various countries

Mick Jagger OGWT special 1970s Loving Cup Jagger
on music, gender and Europe 2016 Jagger / Richards
transformations 1962 -2018 Steve Tyler Brown Sugar
from 2018
Being Mick (Jagger documentary) 2001 Die Stones
laden durch - ein interview mit Mick Jagger und Keith
Richards. Ein Rockpalast Dokumentation von 2005

Soldier Field Chicago June 2019 No Filter Setlist:
Street Fighting Man Let's Spend The Night Together

Tumbling Dice You Got Me Rocking Sad Sad Sad
Bitch Ride 'em On Down Monkey Man You Can't Al-
ways Get Play With Fire Sweet Virginia Dead Flowers
Sympathy You Got The Silver Before They Make Me
Run Slipping Away Miss You Paint It Black Midnight
Rambler Start Me Up Jumpiin' Jack Flash Brown
Sugar Satisfaction
Double Door Chicago 1997 Concert Setlist:
Little Queenie 19th Nervous Breakdown You Got Me
Rocking Crazy Mama The Last Time Anyone Seen My
Baby Out of Control Let It Bleed Shame Shame Shame
Honky Tonk Women Start Me Up Jumpin' Jack Flash
Brown Sugar PLUS Palais Royale Rehearsals 97 Hot
Stuff Mercy Mercy 2019

BIBLIOGRAPHY
For This Book (In no set order)

The Rolling Stones In The Beginning Bent Rej Firefly Books 2006

The Rolling Stones A Life On The Road Jools Holland Avery 1998

The Rolling Stones 50 Jagger, Richards, Wood, Watts Thames and Hudson 2012

Rolling With The Stones Bill Wyman DK ADULT 2002

A Photographic History Of The Rolling Stones Paragon 2012

According To The Rolling Stones Jagger, Richards, Wood, Watts   W & N 2004

50 Years of Rock Howard Kramer Krause 2011

The Rolling Stones Unseen Archives Susan Hill Paragon 2002

Treasures Of The Rolling Stones Glenn Crouch Sterling 2011

The Complete Recording Sessions 1962 – 2012 Martin Elliot   Cherry Red Books 2012

The Rolling Stones Past to Present Tony Jasper Octopus 1976

All The Songs Guesdon and Margotin Black Dog and Leventhal 2016

Rolling Stone Magazine Special Collectors Edition -100 Greatest
Songs 2013

Rolling Stone Magazine Keith Richards Ultimate Edition His Music and Legend 2018

The Best of the Rolling Stones 1963 – 1973 (Vol. 1) Sheet Music

Mojo 40th Anniversary Collectors Edition 2004

241

Mojo Collectors' Series Hot Rocks 1962 – 1969 2019
Mojo Collectors' Series Hot Rocks 1970 – 2019 2019
The Rolling Stones Singles Collection The London Years
- Alfred Music 1991
The First Twenty Years David Dalton Thames and Hudson 1981
History of Rock The Rolling Stones Vol 4 Number 45
Q Magazine Classic and Unseen Rolling Stones
Uncut Magazine Ultimate Music Guide (Issue 4) Time Inc 2015
NME Rolling Stones Ultimate Satisfaction Mark Beaumont 2013
Knebworth Fair Programme 21 August 1976
Der Spiegel Kultur section 21 September 1970
Stoned Andrew Loog Oldham Vintage Publishing 2001
2Stoned Andrew Loog Oldham Vintage Publishing 2003
Mick Jagger Christopher Andersen Gallery 2012
Jagger Carey Schofield Methuen 1983
The Stones Philip Norman Elm Tree 1984
Mick and Keith Chris Salewicz Orion 2002
Life Keith Richards Weidenfeld and Nicolson 2010
Keith Richards Victor Bockris Simon & Schuster 1992
The True Adventures of the Rolling Stones Stanley Booth Chicago Review Press 2000 (originally 1984)
Ronnie Ron Wood St Martins Press 2007
Artist Ronie Wood Thames and Hudson 2017
Old Gods Almost Dead Stephen Davis Broadway 2001
A Stone Alone Bill Wyman Viking Adult 1990
Counting Down The Rolling Stones Their 100 Finest Songs
Jim Beviglia Rowman and Littlefield 2015
The Rolling Stones Chris Sandford Simon and Schuster 2012

Butterfly On A Wheel Simon Wells   Omnibus 2012
Projectmalamute 15 February 2013
Play It Loud: An Epic History of the Style, Sound and
Revolution of the Electric Guitar Brad Tolinski & Alan
Di Perna Anchor 2016
Your Favourite Band Is Killing Me: What Pop Music Ri-
valries Reveal about the Meaning of Life Back Bay
Books 2016
"Why a Rolling Stones bootleg is one of my albums of
the year" John Harris The Guardian. 22 November 2011
"From Squalor to grasping cynicism: How rip off tat for
fans to buy & recreated sixties bedsit show that the new
Rolling Stones show is nothing more than an exhibition
in money making" Toby Young - Daily Mail 6 April
2016
I am Brian Wilson" Brian Wilson with Ben Greenman
DeCapo Press 2016   The
Beatles Tapes From The David Wigg Interviews Oct.
1971
Author Ian Rankin hails anniversary of Rolling Stones'
classic album and reveals why his famous detective Re-
bus could never be a Beatles fan The Sunday Post 23 Sep-
tember 2019
Ultimate Classic Rock magazine " Jaggers final movie?"
Martin Kielty 15 September 2019
Hot Stuff: The Story of the Rolling Stones Through The
Ultimate Memorabilia Collection Welbeck Publishing
2021 Uncut Magazine November 2021 Charlie Watts -
Rock 'n' Roll Gentleman
Far Out magazine "Bruce Springsteen said The Roll-
ing Stones created the 'greatest lyric' of all time" 20ᵗ
January 2022 Joe Taysom

Tribute to Charlie

During one of the many rewrites of various sections of this book, the shock news that Charlie had passed hit the world headlines. He was 80 years old and had been ill enough not to go on tour to the USA for the No Filter Tour. The news, nonetheless, was still a battering ram blow. I was certainly not expecting it and had to check to see if it was really true.

Whenever I have seen Jagger do his band intros, eitherl live or on DVD, before handing over to Keith, for his two songs as lead vocalist during a gig, the level of noise reserved for Charlie was always the most thunderous of all. His almost embarrassed shuffle forward to receive the applause was in keeping with the one Rolling Stone whose lifestyle was the direct opposite to the rest of the group. He never courted popularity and even said he was not really a fan of rock music.

His Jazz background had made him an excellent drummer. Certainly not in the same pounding mould as John Bonham, Ginger Baker or Keith Moon, he nonetheless commanded very high respect. There would be no big flashy drum solos from him. He had the swing. "His innovative use of the snare changed the sound from being mere R & B copyists into something more unusual and sophisticated." (Peter Watts, Uncut magazine November 2021). Charlie's unflashy drumming with recognizable style made him one of rock n' roll history's greatest drummers ever! The thing he was most famous for was his hi-hat "skip." He would usually skip the hi-hat when he played the snare drum that created something special and recognizable in the groove. His impeccable timing was at the heart of all the Stones' music. Jagger said "we are the rock but Charlie is the roll." He was the heartbeat of the group.

I loved the way he played especially the way his right hand used to be raised with drumstick seemingly frozen for a brief second before releasing. As an amateur drummer myself with very few pretensions, I tried to copy this. His playing on songs like *Paint It Black, Honky Tonk Women, Satisfaction, Get Off Of My Cloud, Can't You Hear* Me *Knocking, 19th Nervous Breakdown and Time Waits For No One* are just a few of the highlights of his impeccable playing.

At least we will all get the opportunity to hear his playing again when The Stones do eventually get to finish their latest studio album. This may still be some way off. Charlie had played on a host of songs that will be in the reckoning when the album is finally assembled. The official bootleg style releases of various concerts that are periodically released will still feature his presence.

The number of music stars around the world that gave very moving tributes to him shows how much he was loved and will be missed. McCartney and Ringo from the 1960's closest rivals, The Beatles, spoke of him in very high regard, for example, along with so many more too numerous to catalogue here. I must quote Joan Jett, however, who encapsulated what very many muscicians and fans felt when she posted, "Charlie Watts was the most elegant and dignified drummer in rock and roll. He played exactly what was needed – no more – no less. He is one of a kind."

There are many adjectives that sum up Charlie – all positive and all cool. Whilst being at the heart of the group on stage he had an aura of being in another world where everything was smooth, ordered and completely on his terms.

Throughout Watts' long-running commitment to the Rolling Stones, he mostly rejected the hedonistic lifestyles other members like Mick Jagger and Keith Richards opted for. There was a brief dalliance with drugs and booze in the 1980s but he was able to put a stop to this especially as Shirley, his devoted and long standing wife of 57 years, was on the brink of leaving him. He was probably a Mod before they became fashionable with his love of suits and his smart appearance. Throughout his lifetime, Watts acquired "several hundred suits," just as many pairs of shoes and countless custom shirts and ties, the *New York Times* reported. He even bought forner king Edward VIII's clothes at a Sotheby's auction in Paris. He had them adapted to his own style and frequently wore them. To quote the Kinks, he was a "dedicated follower of fashion" and always stood out in the group photographs.

Charlie also loved classic cars but the irony was that he could not drive. He used to like to sit in them. He never had a driver's licence yet still owned some of the most iconic cars in the world. During the course of his time with the band – almost sixty years, he amassed an impressive collection of classic cars. As an art student in 1960, Watts is reported to have said, "I don't particularly want to drive, but if I were a millionaire, I would buy vintage cars just to look at them, because they are beautiful."

As the "Sunday Times" Rich List every year attests, he certainly became a millionaire, and did buy an array of vintage cars. One of the oldest members of his collection was a 1937 Lagonda Rapide. One of just 25 built, the V12 Rapide was a rare site when it was new, even rarer today. Lamborghini has been the ultimate prize of many rock stars for decades. So, it was only natural for Watts to have a bright yellow Miura S in his stable. These cars would remain in pristine condition.

Charlie and Shirley lived on a farm in the village of Dolton in Devon.

They owned Halsdon Manor, a 600-acre 16th Century estate where they bred Arabian horses. Each Arabian horse at Halsdon was given utmost care with superior, intuitive husbandry. The Watts always believed that proper scientific methods and care would lead to superior breeds of horses. They were very highly respected in the horse breeder's circle and in the village, especially, too.

His link with classic cars and horses completely emphasised his role as a non typical rock star.

There are many stories about rock stars particularly in the early days wrecking hotel rooms. Indeed there is filmed evidence of Keith dropping a TV set out of a hotel window to the pavement far below. Charlie's reaction to hotel rooms was to use his graphic art training to make sketches of all the rooms he stayed in. His training as a graphic designer, influenced the Stones in two ways: album covers and concert stage design which he closely worked on with Jagger.

The album cover for *Get Yer Ya-Yas Out* shows Charlie in a most uncharacteristic pose. He is leaping in the air with a guitar held aloft in each hand and smiling. He is positioned next to a donkey that has a bass drum strapped to each side. He is wearing all white with a Tee Shirt that has a woman's breasts on the front. He also sports a red and white striped top hat that Mick Jagger used on stage. David Bailey, the renowned photographer was responsible for the photo shoot. He filmed it from up a ladder. The shoot can actually be seen in the movie "Gimme Shelter". It appears to be a dark and dank day and one shot shows him riding the donkey with a white cape, red scarf, a knight in armour's helmet and carrying a musket. Charlie does appear to be out of his comfort zone but he grins and bears it. The effect is to present an iconic album cover starring just Charlie to represent the group.

One story which I love, and which is often quoted, is the time he punched Mick Jagger in the face.

Mick and Keith, on tour with the Rolling Stones in Amsterdam, had been out drinking till 5 am and Mick decided that he wanted to see Charlie. He was certainly drunk. He called up to Charlie's room and demanded "Where's my drummer?"

According to Keith, "There was a knock at the door. There was Charlie Watts, Savile Row suit, perfectly dressed, tie, shaved, the whole fucking bit. I could smell the cologne! I opened the door and he didn't even look at me, he walked straight past me, got a hold of Mick and said, 'Never call me your drummer again.' Then he hauled him up by the lapels of my jacket and gave him a right hook."

The follow up is not as well known. Charlie's right hook was no laughing matter, and Mick flew back onto a platter of smoked salmon and began to slide out the open window toward the canal below — Keith realized that Mick was wearing his jacket - one he lent Mick and the one he got married in. Keith hauled Mick back into the room. Charlie was angry, to put it mildly; he would have been happy to see Mick go flying out the window. In fact, he wanted to have another go at it, but Keith was insistent about not wanting to lose the jacket. "Remember, you are my singer!" was Charlie's final comment.

In recent years, Watts had dealt with some health issues, including his 2004 throat cancer diagnosis, from which he "successfully recovered" At the time of his death, Charlie had stepped away from Rolling Stones' summer tour to heal from unknown medical procedures, per his earlier statement (via the New York Daily News). "For once my timing has been a little off. I am working hard to get fully fit, but I have today accepted on the advice of the experts that this will take a while," Watts said. It was these words that made the news that he had passed all the more difficult to take. I, most certainly, had not expected it.

At the news of Charlie's death, Mick Jagger posted a photo of himself with a smiling and laughing Charlie Watts. Keith took a different approach. He posted a Watts' drum kit picture with a sign hanging from one of the stands which read "CLOSED." There was no need for any words.

The Stones began each leg of their 2021 No Filter tour of the USA with a filmed tribute to Charlie which was rapturously received each time. A fitting tribute to a genuinely well loved man.

Thank goodness for recorded music in its various forms and for You Tube, as we will be able to hear and see Charlie in all of his glory whenever we want.

Gone but never forgotten. Never forgotten.

Postscript

We held a pedalo debate recently here in Stoupa, Greece (a balloon debate but in a different vehicle) and I was allocated the role of Poseidon God of the sea, earthquakes and horses. It was my role to dispense with the characters as they fell from grace in the pedalo one by one. In this role I kept thinking of one song only: HEY YOU! GET OFF OF MY CLOUD

Thank you Rolling Stones

Post Post Script

The dangers involved in writing such a book are that things keep changing. As I was about to submit this book for possible publication the Royal Mail decided to get in on the act. After 60 years the Rolling Stones have been commemorated with special issue stamps. I could not let this pass. Of course I obtained several different sets of the fine looking stamps.

These erstwhile rebels who upset the older generation with their long hair, their raw, loud rock music, womanising and drug taking are now presented as part of the establishment. I am not sure what Keith thinks about this. He certainly disapproved of Jagger's knighthood. To me, though, it is nothing less than well deserved and helps to make my point about their acceptance in today's society.

The Royal Mail announced that it had issued this special set of stamps "as a tribute to one of the most enduring rock groups of all time". This was part of the tribute to the 60th anniversary of the group. Who would ever have envisioned that in 1962 or 1972? They were still very much the rebels of the established order and beyond. The banning of *Undercover of the Night* in 1983 is testament to this, for example.

The stamps featured the individual members of the group including Charlie (see below) performing at different concerts around the world from Hyde Park in 1969 to East Rutherford, New Jersey in 2019.

"Few bands in the history of rock have managed to carve out a career as rich and expansive as that of the Rolling Stones," David Gold, Director of Public Affairs & Policy at Royal Mail, said in a statement.

"They have created some of modern music's most iconic and inspirational albums, with ground-breaking live performances to match." There can be little denying Gold's words. This might seem like a trivial event but this is only the fourth time the Royal Mail have

paid tribute to a music group. Yes, and before you ask, the Beatles were one of this quartet together with Pink Floyd and Queen. I know that stamps today are self adhesive but I am struggling to find an approriate pun that involves either sticky fingers or 40 licks. The Royal Mail have entitled their press release about these stamps "Send It To Me" after a reggae-infused track apparently about a lonely man looking for a mail-order bride. Perhaps they know better.

The Two Ronnies!

Acknowledgements

This book has taken a very long time to come to fruition and has been changed many times. My thanks to my long suffering wife, Sandra, who is not really a fan, for putting up with the time this has taken and for her insights and memories. Our son, Christian, who is a very knowledgeable music fan, has offered much in the way of support, advice, artwork and the unforgettable Ronnie meeting at Primrose Hill. Special thanks to Alex Dyer, my friend, former teaching colleague, rugby team mate and concert goer, who has helped with memories of those Wembley gigs we shared and enjoyed.

I have to acknowledge, too, my brother-in-law, Kim Garcia, for his help in research and suggestions and especially my sister, Barbara Russell, who regularly sent me clippings from newspapers and magazines over the years.

Two other friends have helped a lot with the text as they have read versions of the book. Sandra Burrows, who is a big Keith Richards fan, helped tremendously with advice and proofreading especially early on. I would also like to thank Theresa Stoker, who is not particularly a fan of the group but managed to offer a lot of constructive criticism with regard to content and structure - much of which I was able to act upon.

Thanks, too, have to go out to the group itself who have shaped my musical life in so many ways. They may have sung *You Can't Always Get What You Want* but I like to think that sometimes you can, in that they have helped me to gain a great deal of what I have today.

List of illustrations

My Dansette record player, 17
Dave Foxley's Party, 20
Rolling Stones First EP (my copy), 21
The infamous *Blackand Blue* poster, 26
Bill Wyman in conversation outside Cambridge Corn Exchange, 34
God v Mick Jagger Balloon Debate, 72
Who breaks a butterfly on a wheel? The Times, 82
It's Only Rock and Roll drawing, 86
Ronnie and his lover Daily Mail, 88
Rolling Stones ticket Earls Court 1976, 90
Stones Wembley Concert information sheet, 96
Stones Wembley Concert 'Do You Know?' sheet, 97
Stones rumor in Banff Calgary Sun, 107
40 Licks poster, 114
Blue Roots CD, 142
Rolling Stones books, 169
Rolling Stones bootleg CDs, 160-161
Homemade DVD sets,162
Rolling Stones memorabilia, 163
Tongue Logos through the ages, 166
Monopoly set and official DVDs, 165
Mankowitz's Red Cage Picture, 166
Mankowitz's original photo, 168
Tee Shirts, 168
70th Birthday presents, 169
Lockdown, 180
Living in a Ghost Town, 181
Screengrabs from *Eazy Sleazy*, 181-182
DVD cover of Stones and adverts, 245
Drum Kit "Closed" posted by Keith, 256
Hey You Get Off Of My Cloud, 257
Rolling Stones stamp with Mick and Keith, 258

Rolling Stones stamp showing Charlie, 259

Index of people mentioned

As there are no chapter headings in this book as such, but section headings instead, this index does not need to be ultra extensive but will hopefully still serve to aid the reader should the need arise.

Adam Boulton,52
Ahmet Ertegün, 127
Andrew Loog Oldham,11,22, 49, 83, 171
Alex Dyer, 91-98, 106-108, 261
Al Jourgensen,13
Altamont,24, 44, 67, 116, 129, 135,149, 198
Anita Pallenburg, 35, 148
Anita Russell, 25
Ariana Grande, 171
Athur Alexander, 21
Athens 1967, 115

The Bachelors, 57
Baggy Alldread, 39
Barbara Russell 138, 255
Barrett Strong 62
B.B. King 45
The Beach Boys,64, 65, 115
Bernie Barker 70
Bette Midler, 85, 126
Billy J. Kramer, 57
Bill Gates/ Sprint, 100
Billy Preston, 90, 121
Black Crowes,108, 109, 152
Black Uhuru, 95, 102
Bobby Darin, 16
Bobby McFerrin, 39
Bob Davey, 28

Bob Dylan, 47, 118
Bulgakov, 134
Carlo Little, 150
Carly Simon/James Taylor, 128
Chris Heath, 59, 84-87, 108, 109, 140, 250
Chris Rea, 154
Chuck Berry, 16, 58, 69, 128, 153
Cocksucker Blues, 23, 24
Country Joe and The Fish, 72
Cynthia Plaster Caster, 27
Cyril Coggan,70

Dave Foxley, 20
Dave Grohl, 180
Dave Honeyboy Edwards, 45
Dave Stewart, 153
Dave Wilcocks, 39
David Bailey, 254
The Dead Beatles, 132
Delia Smith, 67
Del Shannon, 15, 56
Derek Wallace, 16
Dick Taylor/Pretty Things, 57
Duane Eddy, 15

Ed Sullivan, 48
Eric Clapton, 43, 59, 111

Gary Moore, 45
Gram Parsons, 131
Geoff Emerick, 58
George Shattuck, 158
Gered Mankowitz, 167
Great Northern Hotel. Peterborough, 69

Grosvenor Square demo, 72, 75
Gun, 102

Harold Wilson, 51
Howard Stern, 67

Ian Rankin, 66

Jack Dyer, 140
James Joyce 140
Jerry Hall, 35, 143
J. Geils Band, 95
Joan Jett, 251
John Lydon, 116
John / Mary Cole, 170
Johnny Winter, 44
John Peel, 42
Joni Mitchell, 42
Julie Christie/ Donald Sutherland, 148
Junior Wells, 143
Justin Hayward, 63

Kenny & Cash, 79
King Crimson, 42

Larry King, 158
Lenny Kravitz, 153
Lindsay Anderson, 12
London Palladium, 48, 49
Luciana Gimenez, 35
L'Wren Scott, 35

Madeley College/Keele University, 73
Margaret Trudeau, 84

Marianne Faithfull, 35, 59, 78, 80, 81
Mark and Becky, 73
Maroon 5, 38
Marsha Hunt, 35, 43
Martha and the Vandellas, 124
Martin Scorsese,130, 145
Mary Whitehouse, 53
Mayor Daley, Chicago, 76
Melanie Hamrick, 36
Meredith Hunter 129, 135
Merry Clayton/ Lisa Fisher, 104, 130
Me Too Movement, 25
Michael Eavis, 101
Mr Johnson (NAJ),68

Oasis, 153
Oliver Stone, 136
Otis Redding, 108

Patrick Barlow, 111
Paul Buckmaster, 122
Paul Heath, 39, 135, 171-177
Paul Jeffreys, 13
Percy Sledge, 118
Peter Cook / Dudley Moore, 50
Peter Jackson, 67
Pete Townshend, 58
Piers Morgan, 29
Protests 1968, 73, 74

Radio Caroline, 79
Ready Steady Go, 19, 49, 141
The Rhythm Kings, 33

Richard Ashcroft, 171, 172
Rob Bibby,70
Robert Fraser, 24, 78
Robert Johnson, 45

Sandra Burrows, 261
Sandra Heath 69, 111, 113, 115, 140, 167, 261
Santana Abraxas, 85
Sebastian Coe, 156
The Shadows, 15
Simon Wells, 79
Stanley Kubrick, 136
Starsailor, 111
Steve van Zandt, 153

Tariq Ali, 75
Teresa May, 139
Theresa Stoker, 261
Toby Young, 36
Tom Wolfe, 55
Tony Sheridan, 57
Twisted Sister, 85

Vanessa Redgrave, 74
The Vicarage, Park Crescent, 19

Wes Anderson, 146
William Rees-Mogg 81, 82
Will Smith, 135
Wilson Pickett, 65
World In Action, 82

TABLE OF CONTENTS

Preface 7

Introduction 11

The First Stones' Record 18

Controversy 23

Misogyny 26

Liaisons 35

Enigma 37

The first time I saw them: Hyde Park Concert 5 July 1969 . 38

TV Infamy 47

Relevance and Music Style 50

The Beatles or The Rolling Stones? 54

School times: NME story 67

Christmas Party 68

Balloon Debates 69

A Level History Student 71

ROLLING STONES SONG ANAGRAMS 76

The Redlands Drugs Bust episode (February 1967) 77

Toronto 1977 82

My Son Christian and Ronnie Wood 84

Ronnie Wood's autograph.....................................85

1982 Saturday 26 June Wembley Stadium...........................90

Rolling Stones Firsts 98

Wembley Stadium Concert 4 July 1990 101

Canadian Rumours 106

Wembley Stadium Concert 15 July 1995..........................107

Twickenham Concert 24 August 2003: (Forty Licks)........109

Favourite Songs..114

THE ROLLING STONES: MY TOP TEN SONGS...........116

Here goes then..117

My list of contenders (in no particular order)....................118

Time Waits For No One 118

Moonlight Mile..120

(I Can't Get No) Satisfaction.................................122

Beast Of Burden 124

Star Star 126

Gimme Shelter..128

Wild Horses...129

Sympathy For The Devil 131

Paint It Black...135

Start Me Up 137

Jumpin' Jack Flash 139

Blue Roots CD..141

Martin Scorsese's Use of The Rolling Stones...................144

Jagger and Film 146

Tribute Bands 149

London Olympic Games....................................153

Unofficial Archive..156

Some of my general Rolling Stones memorabilia.............164

My 70th Birthday 169

5th June 2018 Old Trafford, Manchester No Filter Tour: (The latest concert I attended)....................................169

Jagger is The Rolling Stones 175

ROLLING STONES SONG ANAGRAMS ANSWERS (from page 78)....................................179

Lockdown..179

APPENDIX A 183

Introduction from a previous TMA (U203 08) which underlined my topic and approach 183

A little later in my introduction (to TMA 08) I listed the songs on the two albums 184

Assignment U203 09 184

BIBLIOGRAPHY 201

APPENDIX B..205

APPENDIX C..215

PITCHFORK: THE MOST TRUSTED VOICE IN
MUSIC (AN ONLINE AMERICAN MUSIC
MAGAZINE)..215

THE BEST ROLLING STONES SONGS THAT
DON'T REALLY SOUND LIKE THE ROLLING
STONES 215

    "I'd Much Rather Be With the Boys" (1964)..............215

    "We Love You" (1967) 216

    "I Just Want to See His Face" (1972)..........................216

    "Winter" (1973)..217

    "Time Waits for No One" (1974) 218

    "Shattered" (1978).....................................218

    "Dance (Pt. 1)" (1980)...............................219

    "Heaven" (1981).......................................219

    "Too Much Blood" (1983) 220

    "Almost Hear You Sigh" (1989) 220

APPENDIX D 223

BIBLIOGRAPH 241

    Tribute to Charlie 244

Postscript 251

Post Post Script..252

Acknowledgements 255

List of illustrations..257

Index of people mentioned 259

europe books

Finito di stampare
nel mese di novembre 2022
presso Rotomail Italia S.p.A. – Vignate (MI)